Beyond Words:
The Successful Inclusion
of a Child with Autism

Mary Donnet Johnson
Sherry Henshaw Corden
William Allen, Ph.D., NCSP

First Edition

merry pace press
Knoxville, Tennessee

Beyond Words: The Successful Inclusion of a Child with Autism

By Mary Donnet Johnson, Sherry Henshaw Corden, and William Allen, Ph.D., NCSP

Published by:
Merry Pace Press
Post Office Box 10204
Knoxville, TN 37939 U.S.A.

Toll-free: 888-401-BOOK (2665)
Fax: 865-971-4286
www.merrypacepress.com

ISBN, print ed. 0-9753491-0-4
Copyright © 2004
Printed in the United States of America

Library of Congress Cataloging-in-Publication Data

Johnson, Mary Donnet
Corden, Sherry Henshaw
Allen, Dr. William

An account of the positive experience of a child with autism in a typical public school kindergarten class, as seen from various perspectives, with tools and practical suggestions for fostering inclusion in the classroom.

First edition
Includes appendix of forms and suggestions for inclusion materials and a list of resources.
ISBN 0-9753491-0-4
1. Education (general)
2. Special education
3. Autism
4. Non-verbal communication and ways to build academic/social skills
5. Group dynamics/psychology of interaction between typical and special-needs
   children in a regular kindergarten classroom

Book design by Richards Design Group, Inc.
Graphic elements by Stacy Southwick
Authors' photo by Kreis Beall

Table of Contents

DEDICATION v

PREFACE vi

HOW TO USE THIS BOOK..viii

ACKNOWLEDGMENTS xi

CHAPTER ONE
   Premonitions and Preconceptions 1

CHAPTER TWO
   The First Day 15

CHAPTER THREE
   Getting to Know You..29

CHAPTER FOUR
   Finding a Way to Work Beyond Words...49

CHAPTER FIVE
   The Social Maze: Learning to Become
   a Member of the Community 71

CHAPTER SIX
   A Break in Routine: Holidays,
   Disaster Drills and Everyday Upsets..87

CHAPTER SEVEN
   Environmental Issues and Sensory Strategies....................................101

CHAPTER EIGHT
   Making Friends and Moving On...119

EPILOGUE 139

APPENDIX: Inclusion Facilitation Materials..141

RESOURCES 169

About the Authors 171

"Children love to belong."

Fred Rogers
Mister Rogers' Neighborhood

Dedication

This book is dedicated to the memory of
Suzette Williams, teaching assistant at
Rocky Hill School, whose all-encompassing
love of children and cheerful greeting,
"Hi Cuddle-Bug," made *every* child feel
included and accepted.

Preface

Inclusion is a slippery concept — at least as it plays out in most schools today. There is the law. There is the letter of the law. There is the intent of the law. And there is subversive benevolence going on in every single place where people care more about the child in front of them than the law on the books. And that's how this story begins and continues and will go on forever as long as there are people who believe that the word "special" applies to *all* children — those protected by law, and those who are privileged enough to help make the laws of inclusion a living reality.

None of us will ever know exactly what goes on in the mind of a nonverbal child. Not teachers, not friends, not psychiatrists, not brothers, sisters, cousins, or parents. We can guess. We can hope. We can look for small signs of assent or dissent, but we will never really know what a child's experience is until they can express it to us in words. And even then, the report is colored by all kinds of emotions and assumptions that may still obscure the truth.

Starting kindergarten is fairly scary for just about anyone. It is the rare child who bounds out of bed that first day of school and strides into a new classroom full of new faces and new expectations with total confidence. Imagine how it must be for the child who cannot tell us his fears, ask questions or express doubts. Think of the agony a parent feels not knowing if a new teacher can be trusted with this fragile little being, whether or not the other children will accept their non-typical peer, or worst of all, whether or not the child in question will behave in a manner that will invite acceptance.

A parent whose child with special needs is being mainstreamed into a typical classroom has to wonder what the other parents will think. Will they be resentful or kind? Will they make attempts to embrace or ostracize the family that introduces a challenging child to a classroom of typically developing peers?

And then there are endless worries about the child himself. How will he or she manage a curriculum that is rich with new language and songs, social interaction and games, when words are not consistently used to communicate needs, wants, or thoughts? How will letters, numbers and school routine ever be learned? Will he or she obey the crossing guard? Will he or she be able to tolerate the lunchroom noise and get enough to eat even when the child's diet is severely restricted or there are numerous aversions to food? What will the music teacher do with him or her? How will the gym teacher deal with motor planning and sensory issues? Will the child be able to enjoy field trips, be trusted to run an in-school errand, or ever ask to go to the bathroom independently?

Beyond Words: The Successful Inclusion of a Child with Autism was written to help answer some of these questions, share some strategies that worked, and chronicle the successful integration of a nonverbal child into a regular kindergarten classroom. It is hoped that others — parents, teachers, school staff and professionals — might see how powerful and positive the inclusion experience can be for ***everyone.***

How to Use This Book

Use it because you are curious. Use it because you are apprehensive. Use it because you need a model, reassurance, or some new ideas to help you crack the code of the challenges in your own inclusion situation. This book was designed to comfort the reader, provide insights, and offer some practical solutions to situations that often arise in an inclusive setting.

But please remember to use it only as a jumping-off place. The answers to the challenges of your own situation lie within the people you see every day. Look to the principal who takes the time to get good eye contact and some kind of acknowledgment to his friendly "hello" from the nonverbal child every time he visits your classroom. Look to the parent who loves to volunteer and makes it a point to work with every child, not just the "smart" or the "easy" ones. Look to the custodian who gives a "high five" to the nonverbal child every time they meet in the hallway and offers to give him a ride on his cleaning cart just to get a smile. Then see how you can use the commentary and suggestions we have sprinkled throughout to focus the efforts of the very excellent people who surround you and your nonverbal child every day.

Beyond Words: The Successful Inclusion of a Child with Autism is based on an extended conversation between Sherry Henshaw Corden and me that took place over the course of several months. Sherry was our son Pace's kindergarten teacher and is clearly a master at her craft. When our son started the year he was barely verbal, woefully lacking in social skills and a true challenge. But Sherry eagerly took him on and what happened over the course of that year was, in our opinion, an undeniable victory. The initial intention of these discussions was to dissect the experience and try to figure out what had made it work so well so that we could share some of our tips and secrets with others who might be facing a similar situation.

It soon became apparent that we were not the only players in this drama. From the teacher's aide who greeted the child with a hug and "Hi, Cuddle-Bug" every morning, to the lunch lady who smuggled him extra servings of food she knew he would eat. From the dedicated special-education professionals who devised ways to adapt curriculum, add sensory dimensions to mental exercises, and solve social dilemmas, to the typical peers (and their parents) who exhibited such extraordinary kindness, dozens of people were responsible on a daily basis for creating an environment of true inclusion in that classroom.

So we did some research for another few months and talked to anyone who might be able to offer opinions of this particular inclusion experience. We polled parents, student peers, teachers, school staff and special-education professionals, the gym teacher, music teacher, librarian, principal, and custodians, to name just a few. What emerges is a fugue of fascinating responses which echo and complement, sometimes conflict, but in the end crescendo to a resounding affirmation of the benefits of inclusion.

Hardly any full names are given. Those who wished to give their comments anonymously are identified by only the most general description. These statements, especially those from the nonprofessionals, should not necessarily be construed as advice or taken as instruction. They simply serve to illustrate how it was for one little boy — a boy with autism who could hardly say anything when he first entered a typical kindergarten but whose presence in that classroom changed him forever and marked the hearts of everyone he touched with an experience that goes beyond words.

At the end of each chapter you will find insightful commentary and useful suggestions offered by Dr. William Allen, an experienced school psychologist and child development specialist. My husband and I first became aware of Dr. Allen when he was recommended to us as a good resource for testing Pace's academic and developmental status the year before he was to enter kindergarten. Historically Pace had not been very compliant. He had always been obstinate and combative in evaluation situations and nobody had ever been able to get him very far past the first few moments of any of the standardized tests. We had suspicions, but no concrete evidence that our son had some strengths. But we needed proof if he was ever going to be considered for full inclusion in a typical classroom setting.

It was Dr. Allen's talent, perseverance, and creative techniques for eliciting response that allowed us to see just how many fine tools Pace actually did have in his arsenal. He did it by whispering instead of commanding. He did it by waiting that extra minute so that Pace could decipher the auditory cues he found so difficult to process. And he did it by offering positive feedback and simple deep pressure on Pace's hands that kept him grounded and interested.

We asked Dr. Allen to contribute his commentary to this book in hopes that his insights and suggestions might help others to find new ways to exploit strengths, diminish negatives, and foster communication, interaction, and social success among all the players in an inclusion situation.

In an appendix we offer various templates for materials that were developed to enhance the classroom experience for this particular child but that could be of benefit to any child with communication difficulties who is included in a typical classroom. And, finally, we have provided a list of resources we each found enlightening or useful.

Mary Donnet Johnson

Acknowledgments

I grew up with many brothers and sisters, most younger. Early home videos show that I was often a caretaker for some of them. I think that was the root of my interest in working with children. Ed, Sue, Jim, Terry, Steve, Mom and Dad: Thanks.

The three who taught me the most about child development were not on the faculty at the University of Tennessee. They are my own children, and they all taught me valuable lessons. Thank you, Chenoa, Nocona and Quanah.

I would not have finished graduate school without the support of my wife. She has not only tolerated, but supported my education and my job. She has helped me deal with the hardest lessons of children, and life. Dawn, I love you and I thank you.

I try my best to learn from every parent and teacher I work with. I have learned from Mary and Sherry, and I am grateful for the opportunity to work with them. Mary created this project, nurtured it, and made it a reality. Thank you, Mary and Sherry.

Every child has some valuable messages for us. I try my best to learn from my clients. They have helped me decipher some of the endless mysteries of autism, and they have shared with me the miracles of child development. I am blessed to have the opportunity to teach them, and learn from them.

Pace is the star. He is the reason for this project. He worked much harder than I. And, as we finished photographs for this book, he took my hand and intertwined his fingers with mine. Pace, thank you for holding my hand!

William Allen, Ph.D., NCSP

Throughout the book when I say "I," or "we," I refer not to myself alone, but to the inclusion team and to some who came before:

I owe a debt of gratitude to my mother, Virginia Henshaw, who instilled in me from the beginning that the only acceptable way was to include everyone.

To my children, Spencer and Laura, who are my heart and who through my fascination with their educational process lead me to my profession.

It was A.J. Dent who with open arms welcomed all children to Rocky Hill

School insisting that not only is inclusion the law, but the right thing to do as well.

And without Dana Kenny, the "Queen Bee," where would any of us be? She has the knowledge, the foresight and the strength to keep us all going. I would follow her off a cliff blindfolded.

To Beth Morganegg, our speech clinician the year we had Pace in my class, who with only one year's experience, jumped right into a full inclusion program with gusto. To Lynne DeBolt, our occupational therapist, who did come in early so that Pace could swing before school each day. Special thanks also to Sandy Baugh, another school occupational therapist who skillfully incorporated many of the OT strategies we developed one-on-one in the midst of everyone, right there in the classroom Both these talented professionals understood that inclusion means not leaving the classroom unless absolutely necessary!

And Emily McSpadden, a first-year special education teacher with a particular interest in autism, who allowed her brain to be picked and who pitched in any time and in any way she was asked. You saw that what we lacked in experience we often made up for with enthusiasm!

My team mates: Suzanne Davis, Sally Goetting, Carol Phillips, and Kim Rhode. They support me in any and all endeavors and accept me with all my eccentricities without question.

And a badge of courage to Barbara Sanders who after twelve years away from the classroom came back to team teach with me in a time of great change in the world of education on top of a full inclusion class.

The bottom line is Marilyn Hodge, who with style and grace implements what others have decided. No child with Mrs. Hodge has ever been left behind. She truly gets the children's choice award. Just ask them.

To the parents of my students whose faith and trust honor me and whose joy and enthusiasm revive me each fall.

Of course, to my students who want to accept as well as to be accepted if only given the opportunity. They bring light into my life each day.

And Pace, we both learned a lot.

Sherry Henshaw Corden

Pace would never have been as successful at school if he hadn't had the depth of support he has every day at home. A mother's love and dedication should be almost automatic, and with me, I guess they are. But the kind of commitment, ingenuity, and belief in his abilities that he receives from his sister Mary Margaret who is only 15 months older than he, and the endless patience and resources that are continually and selflessly given by his father, Rick Johnson, are nothing short of heroic. Together, we make a pretty good team, and I am privileged and proud to be a member.

Now, as we continue on this journey at school, I see that we would have had a completely different path if several people had not given significant help along the way. We must thank Teresa Vaughn, Lynne Harmon, Kathy Boling, Martha McClellan, and Gina Steinsberger Burch for helping to prepare Pace to enter the regular classroom.

We must also acknowledge our Principal, A.J. Dent, Dana Kenny, Lisa Light, Jan Henderlight, Beth Morganegg, Lynne DeBolt, Sandy Baugh, Mrs. Barbara Sanders, the late Suzette Williams, and the incredibly kind and resilient Mrs. Marilyn Hodge for believing in Pace's potential, and hanging in there with him through the challenging times.

Dr. William Allen was the first to successfully test Pace. It was through Dr. Allen's testing that we found out how extraordinary Pace's strengths really were and how much promise his future might hold.

There is no way we can ever repay Sherry Corden. By refusing to see Pace's differences as shortcomings and not allowing herself to believe he was lost in autism, but a boy, just like any other little boy (only maybe more so), she quite literally gave us our son back.

We'd like to also thank Summer Tucker, Jent Luby, Melissa Johnson, Kathy Houser, Angie Smith and the wonderful Mrs. Joyce Jackson, for keeping the faith, keeping the ball rolling, and keeping the miracles coming in all the time since kindergarten. Emily McSpadden has also been a major force for good and continues to help our whole family in countless ways.

Maureen Ritter, CCC-SLP, who worked with us privately as a graduate student, deserves much credit for helping us create systems at home for molding Pace's behavior and boosting his academic progress. We will always be thankful to Cristina and Patrick McNeill for their contributions and for teaching Pace to say "I love you, too."

And, finally, we are so grateful to all the children who were in Pace's kindergarten class and their parents. They were the true teachers and saints and guiding lights.

This was a story that was a privilege to tell. Thank you to all the friends and professionals who lent their talents and sensibilities to reading our manuscript so that we could refine the telling. Nancy Franklin, inclusion specialist in California, Lynne Harmon, Teresa Vaughn, Angella Crabtree, Emily McSpadden, Sandra Greear, Nikki Burnette — all autism and school professionals here in Tennessee — and Rocky Hill parents Jennifer Carter, Ellen Sullivan, Sis Myhre, and Becky Ragsdale. We appreciated all of your comments and all of your support. Many thanks to Michael Richards of Richards Design Group for making our book *look* so good. Special thanks to Loretta Lang and Terumi Saito for keeping my personal life and professional affairs on track.

And deepest thanks to my parents, Carolyn and Pierre Donnet, who have always demonstrated perfect love — the kind that remains steadfast and true, applauds every honest effort, and bravely smiles in all kinds of weather.

Last, but certainly not least, Pace. Ah, Pace. I can't wait to tell the sequel.

Mary Donnet Johnson

Chapter One

Premonitions and Preconceptions

Pace, on the first day of school at Rocky Hill.

When you send your child to kindergarten you pray he will be safe. You pray he will have friends. You pray that he will learn something and have lots of fun. If your child has autism and is about to enter a classroom full of typically developing peers, you want all these things, too, while at the same time chanting another, more private mantra.

> *Don't let him wet his pants because someone forgot to take him to the bathroom.*
>
> *Don't let him fall on the floor screaming and kicking because he doesn't like the feel of paint on his fingers or the buzz of the intercom.*
>
> *Don't let him hit, pinch or bite the teacher or — heaven forbid — another child because someone gets too close, asks a question, or announces something as simple as "time for lunch."*

Parents whose children with autism are included in a regular classroom often experience an enormous amount of paranoia, fear, and undying hope. By the time our children are kindergarten age, most of us have guided our families through years of intervention to build skills in our offspring with autism. That may include spending a fortune on private occupational and speech therapy, contracting thousands of hours of Applied Behavior Analysis or other behavior-modification programs, vitamin therapy, chiropractic, dietary transformations, and dozens of other interventions we hope may lessen the effects of autism in our children.

The one thing parents often cannot provide for the child with autism before he or she gets to school is the one thing that has been proven, over and over again, to be one of the most powerful motivators for positive change — a typical peer group. Even if the child has a sibling. Even if the child has a loving and close extended family or circle of friends. Nothing is as potent as a classroom of typical role models who are the same age as the child, as new to the situation as the child, and who have as much invested as the child does in making the classroom situation work to the benefit of all.

Inclusion is not just for the child being included. Inclusion is for everyone. And that is why when it works, it always makes everybody stronger.

. . . .

What the other parents thought

Question: What were your impressions of and feelings about a child with autism who may have severe communication challenges before you were in a classrom with one?

I was not worried at all.

MT

Never had direct exposure to one. (I was) very if-y and hesitant if it would actually be good for other students as well as the impaired child.

LC

I had never really had any contact with nonverbal children. I had never thought about it.

SB

They are just children that have special needs. Some can work through it and some will have to compensate for it in other ways.

CG

I didn't know how to react to their actions, or how to interact with them.

HM

I really didn't have any feelings on the subject. We try to raise our children to treat everyone the same no matter what the handicap may be.

JH

The very few "limited-verbal" children that I have ever come into contact with I have personally struggled with because of behavior (or should I say "misbehavior") that I could not control. I'm not comfortable when I cannot use discipline techniques or reasoning to change a child's behavior.

BR

I thought that this would be a great experience for my child. I wanted him to know that all people are not the same but are special in their own way. Also, that differences do not make someone better or worse, and that they should never be treated any differently because of the differences.

MB

I've worked in a Child Development Lab for 17 years and we always had children with disabilities in our program. (My son) often had at least one child with a disability in his classrooms there from infancy through preschool. I believe in inclusion and feel there are many benefits for all involved, but I have not had specific experience with a communication-impaired child.

AS

Having a special-ed background, it was fine with me that Pace was in the classroom. I thought it was good for the students to see how everyone is different.

SM

I thought (he) would not be able to get along with the other students.

PR

What the school staff and professionals said

Question: What kinds of expectations did you have when you learned there would be a virtually nonverbal child with autism included in one of the typical kindergarten classrooms?

(I thought) that he would likely be unmanageable, that he would harm smaller children, and have very limited ability.

School Psychologist

I heard he was smart and I wondered if I would be able to reach him, help him, or even make a difference with him.

Special Education Teacher's Aide

I expected him to be in his own world and would probably use aggression to avoid social interaction with others.

School Speech Therapist

I knew Pace previously from his elementary preschool program, and I have that experience to draw on. I felt uncertain as to what Pace's full potential could be. Due to communication limitations, Pace was not functioning where he needed to be.

School Speech Therapist

I feared him.

Special Education Teacher's Aide

My first thought was "how will I be able to make physical education a stress-free environment for Pace?" I love to teach with a great deal of music and 100% participation as much as possible. This was going to be a challenge.

Physical Education Teacher

I was worried about how to connect with Pace.

Special Education Teacher's Assistant

How was I going to work with a child with communication disorder?

General Education Teacher's Assistant

I was very interested because it was an opportunity for me to learn to be a better educator.

Special Education Case Manager

Parent/teacher dialogue

Sherry Corden: When I first found out that I would have a child with autism who was practically nonverbal in my classroom the next year, my first reaction was "O.K! He's coming! Let's get that I.E.P. (Individualized Education Plan) going, bring him on, we're ready!"

Mary Johnson: My husband and I had heard that Rocky Hill Elementary School provided a really great environment for children with special needs and that you were one of the most experienced teachers in that school. We heard you were passionate about inclusion, obviously loved kids, and would fight to get whatever was needed to help a particular child.

SC: Well, that was probably an inflated view. I do believe in full inclusion and I will do anything I can to help children succeed, but as far as Pace was concerned, it didn't take long for me to start worrying. I thought "Are we a match? Will I live up to expectations? Will the parents be disappointed? Will the child thrive or fail? How can we keep from thinking about him as a project? He's a little boy."

MJ: We went to your class. We observed you in action. We saw there were children with special needs obviously co-existing just fine with the other children. We looked into their faces and we saw calm acceptance and excitement about learning. We decided Pace had to be placed in your class.

SC: I appreciated your confidence in me.

MJ: It wasn't easy to get him there, though. If you remember, there were some tense moments and tough meetings with school officials, but, finally, it was decided that Pace would indeed be joining your kindergarten class at Rocky Hill in the fall.

SC: Then they gave me his file right before school started. It was about a foot thick. I was overwhelmed. I thought "I just can't do this. I'll never get through all this paper." And then, when you told me to just put all that away and deal with the child with fresh eyes, I was relieved. Not that I could have ever not read the files, but it was important to me that you thought I didn't need to know his life history to be able to deal with him.

MJ: I didn't want you to know his life history. It was pretty daunting.

SC: That may be, but it was very freeing to know that you trusted me to size him up in person without relying on the reports that said what he was on paper.

MJ: Dr. Allen was really the first one to be able to access Pace's intelligence and strengths. That was one paper I wanted you to pay attention to!

SC: And we did. It was great information and helped us know who that might be "locked up in there."

MJ: Remember how I always said "look into his eyes — there's someone there."

SC: Oh, yes. And once I met him I had no doubt.

MJ: I'm glad to hear you say that now, but we weren't so sure then. We were terrified. As much as we wanted him to be in a regular classroom with typically developing children, we were scared to death that he would act strange, misbehave, freak out, hurt someone, disturb the peace, pee in his pants and get kicked out.

SC: Right, your first question to me was "What will Pace have to do to be kicked out of your classroom?" Well, that was just the farthest thing from my mind. It made me feel like you thought I was an evil dictator and I wanted you to have faith in me and trust me to work for what was best for Pace. When a child like Pace is first introduced into a typical classroom it doesn't always look pretty at first so that trust and faith are so very important.

MJ: Just goes to show how two people can have completely different impressions of the exact same event.

SC: And that you just never know what the other person is really thinking.

MJ: Right.

SC: I finally got to meet Pace the day you brought him to visit me in the kindergarten classroom as I was getting it ready for the first day of school. I had just washed everything, arranged the shelves and cubbies and tacked my signs and teaching tools up on the walls.

MJ: Your tour of the room and response to our fears was very reassuring. You told us that we couldn't know how very normal most of Pace's behavior was for any five or six year old. You said they almost all act up, freak out, hurt someone's feelings, or accidentally hit, trip or bump into each other. You said disturbing the peace was a regular kindergarten occurance, and that for a child, peeing in your pants is practically a rite of passage.

Sherry Corden's kindergarten classroom

SC: Yes! And because of his autism, I told you that Pace might exhibit all this normal behavior times ten.

MJ: That seemed right to us and made us feel a lot better.

SC: So we looked around the room and I showed you all one of the areas I am most proud of — the "family living" space up high in the loft. Few children can resist exploring it. Special permission is required to go there, time spent in the space is limited, and it is an attractive, clean, fun place to go.

MJ: Of course Pace immediately climbed up there, like a flash.

SC: As we talked and I explained my systems and theories, Pace continued to explore. We could hear him knocking around up there.

MJ: It worried us to have him out of our sight because he was still so unpredictable, but we wanted to hear what you were trying to tell us and show us.

SC: We talked about the nuts and bolts of making the classroom user friendly for Pace without making it too distracting for the other children. We came up with some simple visual supports, a personal schedule board to help Pace know what was happening at all times, a small box full of sensory "comfort items" like squishy balls, Thera-putty, a small sock full of sand. We discussed the best spot for him to occupy on the common rug at circle time. Seemed like we were off to a great start.

MJ: So we gathered up our things and went up to the loft to fetch Pace. There he was, standing stock still in the middle of the floor, looking distracted as a puddle formed beneath his feet on the newly shampooed carpet.

SC: You were mortified.

MJ: I was furious. I thought "How could he do this to us at the first meeting with this wonderful teacher, in this perfect room?"

SC: Well, we got you some paper towels …

MJ: I couldn't stop apologizing …

SC: You were so embarrassed over really nothing!

MJ: But we wanted you to like him so badly.

SC: Do you remember what I said?

MJ and SC: "Maybe he just relaxed!"

How will we ever get past the panic of going public?

If your child with autism is facing the first day of inclusive kindergarten tomorrow, then you have passed some of the biggest milestones, although you may not see it today. You have started to come to terms with the fact that your child is not the child you dreamed of during the pregnancy. Your dreams have crashed, and you probably feel it regularly. You may spend most of your time in "emergency mode," putting out fires just to get through the day. And, as the long-awaited entry into kindergarten approaches, it begins to seem less like a milestone and more like a millstone. You feel its weight around your neck. How will you ever get past it?

Your life is not autism, although you may live it as if it is. What can you do to take care of yourself?

Prepare Yourself

First of all, it is time to reclaim yourself. Your life is not autism, although you may live it as if it is. What can you do to take care of yourself? Call a long-time friend, take a walk, ride your horse, swing a golf club or bowling ball, listen to music, make music, draw a picture.

Many of us give up our hobbies when we become parents. If you are to survive this, and future milestones, maybe you should reclaim one of your lost hobbies. If you played guitar, restring it and play it five minutes each day. If you used to paint, ski, carve wood, roller skate, or knit, make yourself do it again. Forget the guilt; you will be a better parent if you have this outlet, this expression of yourself.

Do not be afraid to take others up on offers of help. Most people who offer help will receive abundant rewards in return. Give them these rewards! It does, indeed, take a community.

If you're going to sustain yourself in this way, you will have to rely on a strong support system. This may take the form of relatives, friends, neighbors, or other parents of children with special challenges. If you once got support from a church, now is the time to use that support. Do not be afraid to take others up on offers of help. Most people who offer help will receive abundant rewards in return. Give them these rewards! It does, indeed, take a community.

Prepare Your Child

Your child is facing a new world. How can you let him or her know what to expect? The best way is to visit the school. Maybe the first visit should be after the students have left and the school is quiet. Walk through the routine. Meet the teacher. Visit again and again. Make a photo album. Include all the parts of the school that appealed to the child (i.e. playground, cafeteria, any colorful bulletin boards or signs) and be sure to take a picture of the child's prospective kindergarten teacher.

As the first day approaches, reduce any extraneous stressors. This is not the time to take away comfort objects, or to start toilet training. This is not the time for dental visits or physical exams. Do these early in the summer, not in the few weeks before school. Stick to a comfortable routine in the last weeks of summer break. There is no need to push the child to the brink just before the first day.

In the last few days prior to kindergarten, consider focusing more on the activities that will soon become daily routine. Make a visual schedule with pictures and print, and weight it heavily with the things that happen first and last in the day. It helps a child know how to begin. It also helps to know the things that mean it's almost time to go home.

You have been spending days, weeks, and months preparing the child for the first day. Therapists have worked toward this. Preschool teachers have worked toward this. Although you may not realize it, the kindergarten teacher has worked toward this. It is time to trust that it will be better than your worst fears, and that it will get better with time. It is not unusual for a child with autism to take two weeks to adjust to a major change. Plan for this and expect it to get better after the "break-in" period. You, your child, and the teacher need these powerful, positive expectations on your side.

This is not the time to take away comfort objects, or to start toilet training. This is not the time for dental visits or physical exams. Do these early in the summer, not in the few weeks before school.

11

Promote Positive Expectations

Look at what went well. What made it work better than you expected? What can you do to take advantage of the things that facilitated a good day? Make them a formal part of the program.

Coaches know the power of positive expectations. They use this power all the time. And they know that if an athlete expects to fail then he or she is likely to do so. But if an athlete expects the best outcome, his or her performance will be better. If expectations can impact the physical performance of an athlete, surely they can impact the mood and thinking of a child, his teachers, and his peers.

Your child will sense your expectations. He or she will know if you are tense and worried, or if you are calm, relaxed, and optimistic. The child will feed off of this. He or she is very likely to mirror your level of tenseness or your level of optimism. We want the child to start the day as calm as possible so he or she can perform optimally.

You will spend time with worry and fear. It is nearly unavoidable. So set a timer and spend 10-minutes sessions envisioning the *best* scenario. Picture yourself on the way to school smiling and positive. Picture your child matching your mood. Recall episodes when your child performed better than you expected. Repeat a positive mantra such as "We've done our best to get ready, so we can enter calm and steady." Tap the power of positive expectations.

Process the First Day

After the first day, take some time to debrief, perhaps in conversation with a relative, a friend, and/or the child's educator. Look at what went well. What made it work better than you expected? What can you do to take advantage of the things that facilitated a good day? Make them a formal part of the program. Use them to build your optimism and support your positive expectations.

Also look at the things that need special attention. What changes are needed? What can you do to minimize the negative factors? Most importantly, process the feelings, as you did in preparation. Let the millstone come off your neck, now! You made it through this feared day. You and your child will make it through tomorrow as well.

How to Define Autism?

Early on, just before Pace was to enter kindergarten, I was involved with his team as they worked to create his educational plan. At one of those meetings Rick Johnson (Pace's father) aptly said that the frustration of trying to help a child with autism was "like dealing with an enigma wrapped in a mystery." Indeed, this is precisely how it feels to most of us who are trying to solve the puzzle of autism as we endeavor to help the children, families, and school personnel who are at the affect of the condition. But even though it may be true that what we *don't* know about it far exceeds what we do know, there are a few things about autism that we can say with assurance.

Autism is a neurological disorder that disrupts a child's ability to deal with the information taken in by his or her senses. Pain comes from sensations most of us hardly notice. Fascination comes from other sensations the rest of us may find boring or monotonous.

Autism interferes with communication. All children with autism have some level of language impairment. Some are nonverbal. Others use language oddly. Some may echo others, repeat themselves, quote movie scripts or respond in the most tangential way to questions.

Children with autism all have difficulty socializing. Some avoid others altogether. Others like to be with people, but don't seem to understand appropriate social interaction. These social issues may be a direct result of the sensory problems and language deficits.

Autism is not hopeless. Children with autism are not unreachable. Children with autism can learn and can improve dramatically. They can live and work independently.

Autism doesn't have to be a barrier to inclusion. Children with autism have the right to an opportunity to join society. Even an "enigma wrapped in a mystery" deserves a place in kindergarten and can, in fact, bring a freshness and diversity to the learning environment that could be of benefit to all.

"It gets you all frustrated to make friends
with people who don't talk."

Morgan T.
Kindergarten classmate

Chapter Two

The First Day

Pace, entering the kindergarten classroom as Sherry Corden greets her new students and their parents.

Parent/teacher dialogue

Sherry Corden: You know that at Rocky Hill we have a tradition of introducing the children in our kindergarten classes to school in small, staggered groups.

Mary Johnson: Right, you have anywhere from three to five different children coming every day for a week until all have had a chance to meet the teacher, familiarize themselves with the routine, and get comfortable with the room.

SC: Letting the children get accustomed to the classroom in small groups at a time also lets us pick up on any potential difficulties and be more attentive to each individual child.

MJ: It's critical for the family of a child with special needs. We came every day, I remember, so Pace could meet all the children and have extra time in the room.

SC: I pretty much do that with every child with special needs. It helps to keep drilling the routine with each new group until some kind of comfort level is achieved.

MJ: I probably didn't dare tell you this, but when we brought Pace to kindergarten for the first time he was still in pull-ups, was not sleeping well, was only eating from a narrow repertoire of choices, was still hitting and kicking when frustrated or afraid, and was just about completely nonverbal.

SC: I did assume that, actually. But I also knew he had tested exceptionally high in certain areas.

MJ: Right, but he still couldn't draw or write, play games, sing, follow any but the simplest directions, or interact with his peers.

SC: He could count, say his ABCs, and judging from the wide variety of books and magazines he seemed to enjoy, don't you think he was reading pretty well by then?

MJ: Oh, probably. He was O.K. on the playground, but still clumsier than his classmates with all the equipment and not at all interested in playing any of the typical playground games.

SC: He preferred to walk the perimeter and sift the mulch through his fingers.

MJ: Which we really didn't want him to do; not to excess.

SC: And let me tell you, whenever it rained he had a great time with the mud and especially liked to get it in the treads of his sneakers so he could pick at it all the rest of the day.

MJ: Safety was an issue. We were afraid he would wander out the door one day and never be found again. We thought he might hurt himself, a teacher, or one of his classmates because he was so aggressive and noncompliant. We thought that all the children would think he was just too weird and avoid him, that the teachers would dread trying to teach him, and that he would come to hate going to school because there was really nothing in it for him.

SC: It wasn't like that at all. We have concerns about almost all of the children at first. Keeping the room orderly and our systems enforced is a major focus of the first few weeks for everybody.

MJ: Well, how do you keep it from being pandemonium?

SC: I have learned to put red circles on certain items in the room that I don't want the children to have access to at first. That might be Work Jobs, the loft, or the door to outside. I do this so I can teach them little by little what the boundaries are as well as how to use each piece of equipment or learning tool and put it back properly each day. This is the only way to keep the room in order and with fewer choices available it also helps make the environment less overwhelming to the children,

MJ: … and their parents.

SC: Yes. But what you didn't know was that although I had had many other children with special needs in my classroom during the seventeen years I had been teaching kindergarten, I had never had a child exactly like Pace.

MJ: Is that why you asked me to be so involved at first?

SC: Yes! I wished I could have a transplant of everything you knew about Pace from your mind to mine! It was such a luxury to be able to just look up and ask you "What does he mean by that?" because I knew that I would never know your child as well as you do and be able to read the signs as well.

MJ: Especially when he was agitated!

SC: Well, yes. But it was so strange. At first I thought he was very unique and would be different from the rest of the children.

MJ: Wasn't he?

SC: Superficially, yes, because he had so much trouble communicating. But after a very short while I realized he was just like everyone else, only times ten. You'd say he'd do all these weird things and I'd listen and think to myself "That just sounds like any other kindergartener to me, only more so."

MJ: When Pace was screaming and the other teachers nearby saw me there every day, what did they think?

SC: They were very supportive, but sometimes I think they thought I was crazy. They'd ask me "Doesn't it make you uncomfortable having a parent watch you right from the beginning?"

MJ: Meaning me.

SC: Yes. But I was glad you were there, and as time went on, I was really glad not so much because you could help me understand Pace, but that you could have the opportunity to work with the other children and see just how wide a definition "normal" can be!

MJ: You're right. It was mind-blowing to me to see the problems some of the other "typical" kids had with learning. It did make me feel a lot better and more hopeful about Pace, because in that context his strengths became as obvious to me as his shortcomings.

Even the smallest gesture of kindness can make a big difference.

SC: The truth is, the minute you start to have success with a child like Pace, or any child for that matter, you want to top it. When you glimpse what might be possible, when you have faith in the child, when you hang in there with the program, and your expectations for success are fulfilled — that is so powerful.

MJ: It was powerful in your classroom, with you and all those great kids who were so kind to him and patient with him and all the many dedicated people dodging his kicks and pushing him to perform. Even when he was crying, flat on the floor, looking demented and totally out of control, because he was in your classroom and everyone was committed to keeping him there, that's when we first began to dare to have hope for Pace.

SC: Yes, and that's what you had every right to feel and exactly what we wanted you to feel. However, I have to admit that for the first month or so, every day after school I'd go home and immediately take a nap.

MJ: Please don't tell me he wore you out that much?

SC: Oh, no. To tell you the truth, I've always done that. No, having Pace in the class provided me with lots of food for thought — things to wonder about and build on — a great challenge. The older I get the more I enjoy those things.

. . . .

What the other parents thought

Question: What did you think of Pace when you first met him?

I thought "What a beautiful child." I was so happy to see his mother enjoying his success in the class.

MT

Wow, what a beautiful boy! I wanted to communicate with him. I could tell he was a very bright child.

SM

Precious boy with beautiful red hair.

DM

I thought he was cute.

DM

I thought he was quiet and well behaved.

MB

At first I was concerned if (my son's) education would be negatively affected. But soon realized the situation taught him things for the real world.

LC

I wondered if Pace could handle the classroom environment.

PR

I had no fears or concerns whatsoever for my daughter. I trust Sherry Corden 100%.

JH

I was curious. How did his mind work? What was he feeling? Was there any chance he could "outgrow" this condition? I wanted to do something to help him. I felt sorry for this sweet little boy who just looked lost.

SB

Sweet. In his own world. Comfortable in the room most of the time.
I didn't have any fear because one of my other children went through elementary school with an autistic child and it only made him more well-rounded.

HM

(My daughter) came home the first day and told us about Pace. Mrs. Corden had explained to the class that he had difficulty talking and what some of the things he did meant. She said that if Pace hit her, she was just supposed to say "I don't like that." I thought the teachers set the standard and Pace was just accepted right away. I was glad for Pace to be there. I like the fact that (my daughter) is meeting all different types of people, no matter what their special need, religion, nationality, etc. at Rocky Hill.

CG

Pace was very quiet when I first met him. He was having a very good day. I was so proud of every child in the classroom and how Pace fit in so well.

JH

He just looked liked an excited kindergartener to me. Pretty normal.

CG

I already knew Pace through church. I was tickled to have the Johnson family among the Rocky Hill family.

BR

What the school staff and professionals said

Question: What was your first impression of Pace?

My first encounter with Pace left an impression of fascination.

CDC Case Manager (and informal
consultant to kindergarten teacher)

I thought he was probably bright, yet overwhelmed and frustrated by the over stimulation.

Occupational Therapist

Smart, strong willed, funny.

School Nurse

That he entered class as a willing worker — cheerful and ready to try.

Music Teacher

Handsome and bright.

Principal

A very handsome little boy.

Librarian

I thought he was a very handsome young man, but I prayed his behavior would get better so he could learn.

Special Education Teacher's Assistant

Beautiful child. But I felt he was "locked up" inside himself — if only I could "unlock" him.

Special Education Case Manager

I felt that Pace was very much "in his own world" and used his aggression to avoid social interactions with others.

Speech Therapist

I thought "Here's a very smart boy." Would I be able to reach him, help him, or even make a difference with him?

Special Education Teacher's Assistant

Before I ever met Pace and put a name and face together, I saw him kicking a staff member in the hallway and gave him my usual "consequences/expectations" speech before it was explained to me that his special need was autism.

A.J. Dent, Rocky Hill Principal

· ·

Exerpt from
Pace, Up Close and Personal
by Mary Margaret Johnson (Pace's sister, then age 9)

2
My Life at Rocky Hill

My life at Rocky Hill began on the first day of school. I wasn't used to all the hustle and bustle of Rocky Hill, so I pitched a fit. Mr. Dent, who at the time didn't know that I was Autistic, walked up to me and said, "Young man, what is the meaning of this?"
"Well", said my dad, "I don't think that he's going to answer you. He might, but I'm pretty sure he won't."
"Well, why not?"
My dad explained about me being

Autistic. Mr. Dent said that he understood, so we made our way to my kindergarten classroom. My dad got me settled in with my classroom and my new teacher, Mrs. Corden. I had a pretty hard first day, but as the year rolled on, I became more and more familiar and happy in Mrs. Corden's class.

O.K., we're here. Now what do we do?

Extend Yourself.

Now is the time to cultivate the school as a support system. You support them, they support you. This means you will have to find ways to be a support to the school.

As you would with a friend, draw the teacher's attention to her strong points and successes. The teacher is human too, with human needs and feelings. So begin every interaction with a positive, supportive comment. Let educators know you appreciate and trust them. The school will share your burden, not resent it. They will come willingly if you expect them to. They will resist if you expect them to. Approach this with the right mindset, with an attitude of trust and friendship.

Friends share things in common. Find the common ground you have with a teacher, speech therapist, and principal. You both like country music? You both like old movies? You both have a pet dog you love? Talk about it! Share as you would with a friend. The school is your community, if you cultivate it. As mentioned in the last chapter, support your school in projects unrelated to your child, even if it is just for one day or one afternoon. Shared experiences build friendships.

Trust also builds friendships. Most educators thrive on watching the miracles of growth and learning. Trust that the teacher, therapists, and principal are committed to finding and facilitating these miracles. There are exceptions, but don't be quick to expect the exceptions. Look hard and long for signs that the school wants to help. Write it down, because you may overlook it later. When you find these signs, point them out to anyone who will listen. Miracles should be shared.

Express Yourself

Even if you build a relationship with the school community, you will probably at some point experience strong and overwhelming feelings that may threaten to sink you. Feelings with no place to go become tension and illness. Neither you nor your child can afford this tension and illness. Express these feelings any way you can. Talk to someone. Write it down, even if you destroy it later. Use any artistic talents you have, or once had, to express the feelings. Call a friend. Join an internet chat room. However, resist the temptation to complain about your frustrations in public forums like P.T.O. meetings and internet billboards. Unbridled venting unfortunately just tends to demean your cause, isolate you even more and demoralize anyone else within hearing distance. Rather, try sharing your concerns with the teacher or school psychologist first. Let people know how you feel and give them a chance to bond with you and support you.

Energize Yourself

If you cannot find a good listener, find a counselor. If there is not one in your family, your neighborhood, your school, or your church, then find one in the yellow pages. A good therapist can help you regain lost sleep in a few visits. He or she can help you find an outlet for the overwhelming feelings and can help you channel the energizing feelings. If nothing else, a counselor can teach you a few new stress management techniques.

One of the simplest yet most effective stress management techniques is deep breathing. Slow, deep breathing, with the entire upper body, can increase the oxygen flow to the brain, leading to clearer thinking and better problem solving. You can do this even more systematically by doing yoga or by finding an audio

Feelings with no place to go become tension and illness. Neither you nor your child can afford this tension and illness. Express these feelings any way you can. Talk to someone. Write it down, even if you destroy it later. Use any artistic talents you have, or once had, to express the feelings. Call a friend. Join an internet chat room.

Commentary and Suggestions: Dr. William Allen

One of the simplest yet most effective stress management techniques is deep breathing. Slow, deep breathing, with the entire upper body, can increase the oxygen flow to the brain, leading to clearer thinking and better problem solving.

tape that teaches relaxation. (See "Resource" section in the back of this book for suggestions.) Such tapes are very effective, especially if they teach deep muscle relaxation and guided imagery. If you use a relaxation tape for 20 minutes, three or four times a week for three or four weeks, you will learn ways to release tension, decrease stress, and reduce the risk of stress-related illness. You can't afford not to do this.

This information is relevant to all parents who have a child with special needs. That means fathers as well as mothers. Much of this also applies to siblings.

"Once the children became familiar with Pace and the things that set him off, they came to accept his outbursts and did not let them interrupt their routine to any great degree. Pace could be in the middle of the floor, having an absolute fit, and the children would not only walk around him, but some would just step right over him — like he was spilled milk."

Sherry Corden

Chapter Three

Getting to Know You

Pace with his classroom aide and new best friend, Marilyn Hodge.

Parent/teacher dialogue

Mary Johnson: Tests showed that Pace was very delayed in some areas and way ahead in others. So that meant that although he had some major challenges to overcome, you all decided he was probably a good candidate for and would benefit from full inclusion in a regular kindergarten class.

Sherry Corden: There was no doubt in my mind. He was sweet. He was good looking. He worked hard. I thought he had great potential.

MJ: That meant everything to us. We had our foot in the door. Our greatest hope had come true. We started to have visions of him being able to lead a more fulfilled and independent life with friends, a job, and all the normal happy things life can bring.

SC: To quote your husband, he was "an enigma wrapped in a mystery" that I wanted very much to solve.

MJ: Meanwhile, this sweet, fascinating boy was making our lives a living purgatory. He wouldn't go to the bathroom by himself and had accidents all the time. He would constantly keep us awake at night with his shrieks and squeals and giggles, or by parroting some video soundtrack he was obsessed with, or by babbling streams of unrecognizable gibberish for hours on end.

SC: That's the part I knew nothing about. He would often make inappropriate noises at school, but after the children got used to them, they learned to just tune him out.

MJ: And then there were all the ways he did not connect. At home he barely acknowledged us, would rarely make eye contact, and hardly ever uttered spontaneous speech.

SC: That's where we had an advantage. There are about 600 students at Rocky Hill, and dozens of teachers, and just about everyone takes inclusion personally. Once people were aware that we were trying to improve his communication ability, he could not walk down the hall without several people stopping him every time and insisting that he make eye contact and say hello.

MJ: Well, at home he was mostly still making ugly noises to get what he wanted and melting down to the floor, kicking and screaming when he didn't like something. It was not pleasant.

SC: We got some of that, too, and that's where I felt my greatest lack. I mean, I knew developmental patterns. I knew social growth — in typical children. I had gone to school for that. But autism was not anything I knew a lot about. I wanted you to know that I was going to listen to you and learn all I could, and that I was really going to try to be good to Pace. But I needed your help.

MJ: It was wonderful to see how easily you folded Pace into the kindergarten classroom and how accepted he was by his peers. Up until then we felt that his sensory defensiveness would keep him from participating in and enjoying the world.

SC: From what you had described about the way Pace was before he entered my classroom, I expected he would not be able to tolerate noise, closeness to the other children, textures, smells, and visual stimulation.

MJ: Yes, all that kind of input had made him either shut down or lash out. But you were determined to move him past all that. How did you do it?

SC: We gave him his own spot on the rug just like all the other children, but we made his close to an exit and on the periphery with something solid at his back. I would have much rather had a circle because it's far better for the children to be able to see each other's faces and get more feedback. Unfortunately our class was so large that year with 25 children, I was forced to put them in rows on the rug, and that's the best I could do for Pace.

MJ: I know. And the way you positioned him was good. He had his back to the bookshelf and was only surrounded on two sides with other kids.

SC: Right. He had the door on one side, a child in front of him and a child to the side, and the bookshelf at his back.

MJ: And you kept a box of sensory hand toys in that bookshelf at the ready if he needed to be calmed or kept focused, right?

SC: Right. I had to figure out some simple solutions to help Pace stay "in the room." In public school you have to be careful and creative about dealing with a child like Pace. You can never obligate the system. You can't say "Gee it would be great if the OT could swing him every morning before I get him." I would be in trouble with the OT and the system that has to pay for that.

MJ: But I could ask for that. As a parent I have the right to request services for my child.

SC: Yes, you do, and of course there are never enough to go around.

MJ: Yeah, well, that's another story, right?

SC: Right. So I mainly watched him to see what turned him on and then made myself the keeper of those things. This made him realize I had power and attracted him to me. It didn't take any time at all for him to know that he had to direct his requests to me rather than anyone else — not aide, not room mom, not anyone. And that showed me he had the social structure figured out.

MJ: So that explains how they get things from you. What methods did you use to get things from them?

SC: I have found that if I watch for my opportunities to catch the children doing something good and follow up quickly with a reward they care something about, a lot of learning can take place. It takes a light touch. Almost all of them end up coming around. Pace did, too.

MJ: Remember how you made him "dance" and "sing" along with all the other children during circle time?

SC: Yes. But in that case it really wasn't me. It was his aide, Mrs. Hodge. She was his guide and did a whole lot of hand over hand — actually manipulating his arms and legs to go through the same motions as all the other children. That's how he learned it. And boy, did he enjoy it!

MJ: I was amazed the first time I saw that. He was clumsy, of course, and he wasn't really singing or really dancing, but he was participating more than I had even seen. And he just had this big silly grin on his face like he was loving it.

SC: You should have seen your face. I don't know which I liked watching more — him, or you enjoying him.

MJ: It made me very happy. Seeing him like that used to affect me so deeply, I would leave your classroom with this incredible sense of hope and lightness of spirit. I used to catch myself actually driving under the speed limit after being in your classroom. That wasn't like me. I used to speed like a maniac because I was always in a kind of emergency mode. But suddenly I felt calm and like Pace might be O.K. after all.

SC: I felt very blessed by that. One of the greatest things about teaching is to become a part of people's families. And I have to say the progress he made was very satisfying to all of us. By about half-way through the year he was able to sit close to other children at a row of computers, walk in a straight line down the hall with everyone else, eat at a crowded table in a noisy lunchroom, go to physical education, music and art classes, and participate in all the rituals like calendar, weather, news, as well as curricular demands like Work Jobs and table activities.

MJ: You eventually were able to anticipate his need for bathroom breaks. I think your aide Mrs. Hodge was the first one to get him on a consistent schedule which trained him to "go" at the same time every day. That was a triumph!

SC: And we all got used to the kind of preparation he needed to make smooth transitions. We also purposely switched around his aides to keep him from becoming too dependent on any one person and to give us all the advantage of getting experience with him.

MJ: It was hard for him, but you're right, it did make him more flexible.

SC: That's my most favorite life skill — the life skill of flexibility. That's what it's all about.

Sometimes it takes a little push from a friend to get a guy in the swing of things.

The Learning Curve: Fumbles, Frustrations, and New-Found Friends

The teacher's perspective

At first we did a lot of adapting to simplify the demands and ratchet the requirements down to a more manageable level. Since he had never been able to color or draw up to this point, Pace refused to cooperate anytime we tried to get him to hold a pencil or paintbrush. He'd just "lose it." So instead of drawing a picture to illustrate the letter "B" we had some pictures from magazines pre-cut and we let him choose one or two and glue them into his "pictionary" book. This process became kind of a template for dealing with Pace. If we were asking him to do a non-preferred task it was important to scale down or limit the objectives.

We did a lot of "fill in the blanks" with his work, and allowed him to circle the right answer instead of writing it. He did enjoy tracing and anything that allowed him to push pins or lace or pick up small items with tweezers. That was lucky, because it turned out to be essential fine motor practice for the day when he *would* be able to write. His visual abilities were off the charts, so letter recognition, numeration, and phonics came fairly easily to him.

But overall it was really hard to figure out what he knew. For instance, he was great at sequencing events by placing four cards in the proper order to show the progression of a simple story, but we were pretty sure he didn't have a clue about parts of speech, punctuation, or sentence structure. We were surprised when he appeared to have learned to recognize each child's name from various visual clues around the room and could read and say each one aloud after just a very few weeks. But we could never get him to answer even a simple "yes" or "no" question aloud in class.

When we saw how much any demand on him for performance in front of the others upset him, we tried to lower our communication demands. "Just fill in blanks," we'd tell him "Choose the answer from a word bank — you don't even have to say it, just point to it." And we learned to give him a little more time — a "head start" on a task — and that usually was all he needed to be able to fulfill what was asked and progress academically.

My favorite moment was the day we were doing the "daily news" as a group and I was having the children write as much as they could with chalk on the blackboard. I came to Pace, and mind you, he was not talking much at all. I asked him to tell us about an event I knew had happened to him recently, because I had been told. It was something like he had gone swimming or to the beach. I had the idea to write the words for him with a water pen on the board, and have him trace them in front of everyone. That was a big thrill because he jumped right up, did it perfectly, and loved doing it. Everybody clapped. It was little adaptations like these that made him seem more of an integrated part of the group with real experiences and a real desire to connect.

The parents' view

We started to relax when we saw that the teacher and all the special education personnel were treating Pace with respect while encouraging him to perform more and more each day. We were so happy that they cared enough to keep raising the bar, pushing the envelope, edging him out of his comfort zone and into new areas of growth and ability.

Connections are strongest when everyone is part of the circle.

However, that feeling of joy began to unravel around the middle of the year when all these exciting new demands started to make Pace feel pressured and apprehensive.

He resisted. He became obstinate, noncompliant, and combative. He refused to participate. He would fall asleep at odd times. He was susceptible to every cold and virus. He could be completely peaceful one moment and then erupt into a screaming, kicking banshee the next. We thought the children would surely be afraid of him now, hate him, or shun him. But, no. They still grabbed his hands or forced him to hug. They fought to be next to him in line. If he looked like he wasn't going to return to class from the playground with the others in time, a little posse would always go and fetch him and bring him back to the group.

At the computer, children were fascinated with Pace's ability and would sit on the chair with him, squeezing him from both sides, chattering loudly and crowding him. They noticed how much he liked books and quickly decided he was "really smart" and could "read better than anybody."

But despite all this positive reinforcement flowing his way, time and time again I saw Pace take aim at his classmates. Usually the target child simply moved away, or took Pace's hands and looked him in the eye and said "I don't like it when you do that." This is what the teacher had instructed them all to say to each other when anything bothered them. It seemed that even as difficult as Pace could be, these children had decided to accept him and love him and hold him to the same standard of behavior as everyone else. It seemed to give them great joy to do so, and they were unflagging in their zeal.

One day I was sitting in the back of the room, observing Sherry read a story to the children. All was calm and I was lulled into a feeling of contentment, even happiness, that our son was part of such an idyllic setting. Sherry turned the page. Somebody shifted position on the carpet. Then, for no reason at all that I could see, Pace suddenly kicked the boy in front of him. Hard. I waded through the children and grabbed Pace by the shoulder and shook him. "No! We don't do that!" I hissed. The aide sitting next to him took both of his legs in her arms and swung them away from the other child. Pace sank into himself. Tears welled up in my eyes. The child he had kicked rubbed his back, looked at me, at the teacher, at Pace, and with no expression of anger or even surprise, just edged quietly out of range and returned his attention to Sherry.

I fled the room and found sanctuary, in the nearest kindergarten girls' bathroom.

Sick

I felt like the greatest sinner in the world putting these innocent children in harm's way just so my innocent child might have a chance to be more "normal." And actually, the thing that bothered me the most was not that my child had kicked another child for no reason at all, but that the wronged child, once he saw who the offender was, was totally unruffled because it was Pace, and it was expected. As I cried quietly in the girls' bathroom, feeling so out of place among all the little kid-size toilets and low sinks, I thought: who was I to ever think that he would be anything other than severely disabled, without friends, not teachable, and untrustworthy all his life?

The teacher's perspective:

Well, here's another example of our seeing the same incident in two entirely different ways. You saw a child who was wronged assuming that your child was bad and not even worth comment when he did a wrong action. I see a child who has decided the transgression was just part of something his friend is working on and something he was not going to call attention to, but just deal with. Believe me, if that child thought Pace was evil for kicking him he would have raised his hand right up and told me so.

We all accept the strengths and weaknesses of those we love — in this case our classmates. Pace was allowed weaknesses just like the other 24 children were allowed their particular weaknesses. They know this is something that is being worked on so they will not necessarily call attention to it. It's like passing a house under construction every day. We don't say "well, that's not finished." We know it is being worked on so we don't go out of our way to comment on it negatively.

What the other children felt

In the beginning when he came to kindergarten he couldn't say anything!

Amanda G.

He hitted.

Macy M.

He kicked people when he got frustrated.

Amanda G.

When he was hitting he kinda scared us because we were afraid he might hurt us, and he did sometimes. Well, he didn't exactly hurt. When my sister hits me it always hurts and I thought Pace would do the same thing with the same amount of hurting but he really didn't. He was just upset because we were talking so much.

Jack R.

We'd say "No! Don't do that, Pace. Stop that. Don't hit! It's not good."

Morgan T.

I wanted to sit close to him and be his friend.

Macy M.

Even though he didn't talk I still wanted to play with him.

Peyton B.

Parents' view

Then, later in the year, sometime around Christmas, one night, while giving Pace his bath, I noticed he had scratches under both his arms. How had that happened? There had been no comment, no mention of anything out of the ordinary in his daily report. I placed my fingers over the marks. They fit. These scratches had been made by adult-sized fingers, no question. Heat boiled up into my head, my cheeks flushed and all kinds of ugly images swam in my mind. As usual, Pace was blissfully unaware, happily plunging under the water, blowing bubbles and emerging to gather in air again and again, making his typical squealy-squeaky noises like a little dolphin.

I bathed him, put antibiotic cream on the marks and dressed him in his softest, most comfortable pajamas with special care. Tears stung my eyelids again, but this time, for my son. I knew it couldn't have been his aide. She was pure love and would never hurt him on purpose. I knew it really couldn't have been anyone of the members of his team. He must have done something, or not done something that had caused someone to wrestle with him enough to have unintentionally caused this injury. But, what?

The next day, as I questioned the special education supervisor, I was told that he had refused to go into the gymnasium and that it had taken four people to transport him in with a fireman's carry.

· ·

What the other children felt

Pace didn't like the loud parts in gym.

Ray B.

There's a lot of noise in the gym.

Amanda G.

Screaming.

Macy M.

I was afraid he would flip over when they had to carry him to gym.

Jack R.

I was afraid he would fall.

Morgan T.

But if they didn't carry him to the gym then he would be by himself and with not his friends.

Macy M.

He should be with other people.

Peyton B.

Or he will be sad.

Macy M.

Parents' view

Why did it matter so much? What if he had a head cold or his ears were stopped up and the noise in the gym was unbearable to him that day? He couldn't tell us. He wasn't to the point then where he could even localize any pain in his body and point to it and tell us what hurt. His sensory processing disorder disconnected him from most of the sensations we all take for granted and can identify easily (like headaches, stomach aches, ear infections, etc.).

He could never pinpoint any malady. Whenever he had an ailment it just caused general malaise or stubborn noncompliance until the condition cleared up. I asked them to please examine him closely when he suddenly exhibited unusual behavior. Bring him to the nurse and let her take his temperature. No activity, especially one that is not part of the academic program, should require four people to get him from point A to point B.

Well, they worked it out eventually so that everyone's needs were satisfied. We were told that when Pace finally got into the gym and started activities with the class he waded right in and actually seemed to enjoy himself. So, after that, all the teaching staff really wanted him to go every time. For a while, to get him over the hump, they would commandeer a wheelchair and give him a swift ride down the hall to the gym to help him transition more willingly. Now, years later, gym is one of his favorite destinations, and you would have a hard time telling him apart from all the other children as he laughs, tumbles, and plays, just like everybody else. And there have never been scratches under his arms again.

● ●

What the other children's parents thought

Pace would sometimes become agitated, hit, cry, as a result of frustration. Other than feeling compassion toward Pace, I wasn't worried. The teachers always handled the situation well.

MT

At the beginning of the year I was uncomfortable with how Pace could hinder the rest of the class. When he tried to hit the other children, I kept very reserved until I heard how the children were taught to deal with it.

LC

Once I observed Pace getting frustrated at circle time. Marilyn, the teacher sitting with him, was able to assist him. He was then comfortable and sitting quietly.

MB

The worst thing I ever saw was when he hit his aide when he had a fit. I was sorry the other children in the class had to witness that. They looked confused.

SB

He would kick and scream and want to be left alone. My heart ached for this little guy who was obviously distressed.

DM

It made me sad that he was frightened or angry, but understood that it was his way of releasing some feelings.

DM

I felt for Pace. I knew he was frustrated and especially when people would talk down to him when correcting him.

SM

One day he had a fit and another teacher had to restrain him. I felt sad, and at the same time, I was grateful that my kids are healthy.

PR

I felt worse for the teachers; the kids seemed oblivious.

HM

One day when I was at school, Pace was not having a good day. And he was raising his voice a lot. At first I didn't know how to react, but when I saw the children keep going on with their activities and not let Pace's moments bother them, I was impressed.

JH

I appreciated how open Mary was at the beginning about Pace's special needs. It was helpful to feel a part of helping him — to know what he was working on — speech, inclusion — that he is autistic. And the teachers really set the tone so strongly the kids just had to fall in with that.

CG

I was very proud of how (my daughter) accepted Pace in her class. When she would talk about Pace at home we had no idea what the issues were with him. To (my daughter) he was just another friend of hers that she looked after a little bit more.

JH

I am so thankful for the gift of being able to spend time with Pace and Mary. The entire Johnson family is never far from my heart.

BR

(My son) feels sad that a kid his age is unable to comprehend certain things such as playing a sport. One night in (my son's) prayers he asked if God could please make it so Pace could play baseball, because "Pace hits hard!" (my son) said.

PR

What the school staff and professionals saw

I thought he was challenging, but once everyone learned what he needed and how to work with him, he didn't need to fight because he wasn't frustrated anymore. And then he became a delight to work with.

Occupational Therapist

I was excited about Pace's progress at Rocky Hill! I felt he would continue to learn and develop there. I was pleased to see he had overcome a number of his fears and that the staff worked as a team in order to find the most effective learning strategies for him. I appreciated his involvement with general school activities and the fact that he was provided with all possible learning opportunities.

Speech Therapist

He was so bright and capable of learning and doing so much.

Teacher's Aide

There were times I felt extremely frustrated that he could be his own worst enemy. He was often resistant to new experiences and had so much to learn. I desperately wanted him to be able to communicate his feelings instead of physically reacting to his apprehensions. It was extremely important for him to have structured systems in place.

Speech Therapist

He was sometimes unkind to the other students and it seemed hard for him to understand that this was inappropriate.

Librarian

We have had bad moments, and I have the scars to prove it! The worst part of those times is I felt I let Pace down by putting him in a situation where aggression was his only mechanism to cope.

Speech Therapist

His violent reactions to non-preferred activities were the most difficult challenges. My main concerns were that he would not be accepted, my staff would be injured, peers would be hurt, and his academic progress would be compromised.

Special Education Case Manager

The only problem I had was trying to give instructions to an entire class while Pace was interrupting by being vocal. The students' concentration would be broken and a great deal of repetition would be necessary, but we worked through it.

Physical Education Teacher

The worst moment I ever had with Pace was when he was especially violent and caused me injury by headbutting my jaw.

Special Education Case Manager

The worst moment I ever had was when Pace got mad at me during a sensory activity on the swing and I stopped it and he kicked me in the throat.

Teacher's Aide

There have been rewards, too. One time I said "Pace, you're a neat kid!" He stopped, looked at me with excellent eye contact, and smiled. Those are the moments that make you love what you do!

Speech Therapist

Bruises will heal. There are many ways to achieve a task, and sometimes you just have to keep trying different approaches and keep trying and trying.

Teacher's Aide

It was helpful having Mary at school in the beginning, but it could also be somewhat awkward if Pace was having a hard day. I came to appreciate both of Pace's parents for their confidence in the Rocky Hill staff, especially regarding the staff's commitment to making Pace's educational experience as meaningful as possible. That took both courage and a great deal of trust.

Speech Therapist

Sometimes friendship happens even when nobody is talking.

How do we make this a positive experience for everyone in the class?

First, Identify the Strengths of the Child with Special Needs

**Assessments often reveal a child's hidden strengths.
A good assessment will document strengths first, challenges second, interventions third, and, when it's needed, diagnosis last.**

In our public school system, as a result of the Individuals with Disabilities Education Act, every child with special needs must undergo an assessment to receive services.

Assessments often reveal a child's hidden strengths. In fact, a good assessment will document strengths first, challenges second, interventions third, and, when it's needed, diagnosis last. Some strengths commonly found in children with autism include a keen visual memory, a deep knowledge of facts pertaining to a subject of interest to the child, a highly developed sense of how things work, or an ability to read, solve mathematical problems, or reason that is far above age level.

All children have strengths. Is the family caring and involved? Is the child healthy and well grown? Can the child operate the TV or VCR? Does the child respond to any calming techniques? Can the child align, sort, or match? If you haven't found strengths, lock yourself and the team in a room with no food or water, and let them out when they have a list of strengths. The point is that not having any strengths to list is not an option.

Acknowledge the Challenges and Create a Plan

Some challenges that are frequently experienced by a child with autism are an inability to communicate fluently, difficulty joining and enjoying social experiences, poor modulation of emotion, difficulty controlling outbursts, and odd or atypical focusing of attention.

Interventions that are of the most help are often provided by occupational therapists, speech-language pathologists, and coordinators of special resources who can create a strong plan and pull together the right people for a successful inclusive education experience. Successful interventions also include peer interactions that are guided and fostered. Thus, the crucial importance of inclusion!

Attend to the Suffering

When worlds collide, as they surely do at the beginning of the kindergarten year, there will be rough moments. There will be suffering. In her accounts throughout this book, Pace's mom shows us this explicitly. Many educators work hard to isolate themselves from the suffering. This is done by focusing on the business of education rather than the experiences of education. Sherry Corden describes the experiences. The peer parents describe the experiences. We cannot ignore the experience or the extent of the pain that comes with coping with the challenges. We must acknowledge it, share it, and learn from it. By doing so, recognition of our common "humanity" will allow us to mobilize all our resources.

We cannot ignore the experience or the extent of the pain that comes with coping with the challenges. We must acknowledge it, share it, and learn from it.

Take a Cue from the Children

The peers find it easy to mobilize their resources. They bring an open quality, a fresh outlook, and acceptance that adults find difficult due to our efforts to distance ourselves by analyzing the situation. I think the peers get to the issues quickly, and without pre-existing bias and buffers. The peers show us that they see how the child is like them more than unlike them. They expect to accept him. Not only do they see the strengths, they see the challenges as strengths and admire them. (Patti's son wants Pace to play baseball because he can hit hard!) These peers see the commonality of this child with unique needs. They don't have to modify their expectations and reactions.

The peers show us that they see how the child is like them more than unlike them. They expect to accept him. Not only do they see the strengths, they see the challenges as strengths and admire them.

Commentary and Suggestions: Dr. William Allen

Change the Setting to Change the Child

The adults, on the other hand, need to modify their expectations. The teacher and professionals describe how this happened for Pace. They did not set out to change the child only. They set out to change the environment more than the child, leading to change in the child. A basic tenet of educating a child with autism is: change the setting more than the child. Adapt to him to help him adapt to you. Adapt the setting to help him or her adapt to the setting.

In the process, everyone suffered injuries. The lessons learned were worth it. The child's scratches, although unfortunate, got him into the gym where he learned that it wasn't as bad as his sensory difficulties led him to fear.

Good Inclusive Teaching Pulls Everyone Into a Circle of Learning.

So how do we, and the child, come to face fears of sensory events? We can prepare him and ourselves. We can learn all we can about him and teach him all we can about what is ahead. We can teach him with cues, pictures, homemade books, and visual schedules. Sometimes we can teach by gradual exposure. Always allowing escape will not necessarily help him, just as our escape will not help us. Once he is in the middle of the fear experience, sometimes we will have to force him to face it before he can see that it is not so bad.

If we force the issue, we must do it as calmly and simply as possible. Calmness is important, because our tension will increase his tension. We can push the issue while decreasing task demands. For example, we can lead him screaming into the gym but reduce the volume level and the requirements for participation. Sherry did something similar when she wrote the words with a water pen and allowed Pace to trace over them. She made him deal with public

---

Always allowing escape will not necessarily help him, just as our escape will not help us. Once he is in the middle of the fear experience, sometimes we will have to force him to face it before he can see that it is not so bad.

Sherry made him deal with public participation, but she found a way to change her teaching method so he could learn. The experience was joyous for Pace. Notice that it was also joyous for Sherry! They both experienced success.

participation, but she found a way to change her teaching method so he could learn. The experience was joyous for Pace. Notice that it was also joyous for Sherry! They both experienced success.

Successes and Strengths

Throughout the experience, it is important to attend to the successes, the strengths, and the accomplishments. The peers do it naturally and share the joys by discussing them with their parents at home in the evening. The teacher does it and preserves her sanity. She also gains strength from it. The parent looks for it, fears she will not find it, but clings to it when she does.

Pay attention to the strengths and accomplishments. Don't let the struggles overwhelm you. If they do, as by bringing your tears or by keeping you awake at night, get out your accomplishments list and review it, edit it, and expand it. Ask others to help you (maybe the next day, rather than in the middle of the night). Ask the teacher. Ask the peers. They will teach you what they have learned. Go back and read the peer comments and you will see that they have grown and learned from the similarities, strengths, and successes.

A basic tenet of educating a child with autism is: change the setting more than the child. Adapt to him to help him adapt to you. Adapt the setting to help him or her adapt to the setting.

Pay attention to the strengths and accomplishments. Don't let the struggles overwhelm you.

"I was determined that Pace participate with his class in every way possible, that he adapt to change, that he become more tolerant to new situations, noise, etc. — and he did!"

Special Education Case Manager

Chapter Four

Finding a Way to Work Beyond Words

Pace and friend, John T., tackle some math on the computer.

Parent/teacher dialogue

Sherry Corden: As I thought about Pace the summer before he entered our classroom, it seemed to me that a child who didn't use words would be very reliant on visual cues like schedules, signs, labels, and pictures. We wanted to be proactive so we put up big poster boards on the walls with removable pictures that we could change to show what was going to happen each day.

Mary Johnson: We had visual schedules at home, too. We had a long piece of cloth with seven pockets and in each pocket we would put a mini-schedule of the main events of each day of the week.

SC: We stuffed baggies full of color Polaroids of every person, place and thing imaginable and kept them readily available. We created a stack of portable foam core boards with Velcro strips and picture symbols with Velcro dots on the back of each one to show Pace every class, destination, or event that could happen in any given day. These even included symbols for things like fire drills, early dismissal, special shows and school assemblies.

MJ: We had drawers and shoeboxes full of PECS (Picture Exchange Communication System), Velcro everywhere — in the bathtub, by the toilet, next to the sink — anywhere we needed to show Pace the steps to any task. We cut out pictures from magazines and food wrappers, and took photos of every destination that held any meaning for or might motivate him.

SC: It was too much to keep up with; especially when our hands were already full with a kicking, screaming, often noncompliant child who didn't want to look at anything, much less a visual schedule of activities he really wasn't eager to do.

MJ: Yes, I think we all may have been a bit over-zealous and unwittingly put Pace into sensory overload. We probably didn't realize how exhausting this "school inclusion thing" was on top of his already demanding schedule of private speech therapy, occupational therapy, a home program for his "off" hours that consisted of language-building field trips, play dates with friends, and a long list of on-going self-care/independence-building activities.

SC: I know. Those of us working in the classroom tend to forget the kind of grueling schedule our kids with special needs have outside of school.

MJ: There's really no alternative. We parents of children with special needs have this pressure to do all these things in the early years because we are told that interventions for children with autism have their best impact while the child is still young.

SC: That may be, but I think it's also important for the child to just be a child.

MJ: Well, it was a tough year for us. We tried to build in lots of rewards and "down" time, but it was all a bit much for a little guy who was still not sleeping or eating well. In the few moments we would leave him alone to his own devices at the end of the day, he would typically wolf down several bananas, compulsively play a computer game or watch some video again and again and again. Then we'd bathe him, put him in his room, shut the door, fall into our own bed with a sigh, and spend the next few hours staring at the ceiling while we listened to him jump on his bed, giggling and chattering maniacally until he would finally quiet down around 1:00 or 2:00 A.M.

SC: No wonder he fell asleep on our floor so often!

MJ: Yes! In the morning, after a night like that, we would pull him out of his bed, wash him, wrestle him into his clothes, wedge him still half asleep into the back seat of the car with a bag of Cheerios and a juice box, strap him in and drive him to school. We thought we were doing well if he finally woke up by the time we arrived at school by 7:45 A.M. A few weeks like that, and it was clear that we needed to simplify something.

SC: I think we all discovered that there were enough visual cues in the room already, just as it was normally. I have always used visual reminders for every child in the room for as long as I have been teaching. There are red dots on places and things that are off-limits, various colored dots to show where specific things are kept, charts listing the children in each sub-group of the class (Blue Group, Red Group, Yellow Group, Green Group), and a list of five simple rules that are to be observed at all times.

Sherry's Rules

Always demonstrated with the physical cues indicated.

1. Follow the teacher's first request.
   (Scooping motion of closed hand with index finger pointed upward.)

2. Keep your hands and feet to yourself.
   (Hands and feet splayed out, then folded in.)

3. Ignore inappropriate behavior.
   (Exaggerated motion of head turned to profile with eyes closed and nose in air.)

4. Walk and talk quietly.
   (Elaborate tip-toe.)

5. Raise your hand to speak.
   (Left hand raised. Right index finger to lips.)

MJ: *I love those rules.* I think they should be printed and put on display in every home, business, church, school; whatever — not just kindergarten.

SC: The world would be a better place, wouldn't it? But, anyway, here are a few things that I do for all the children that worked really well for Pace, too.

I sit in my rocker during transition times and signal to each child that they can line up by showing cards with a child's name on each one — one at a time. This encourages reading and name recognition of self and peers.

I have labels and signs on many things in the room, as well as charts to promote phonemic awareness, math, and science skills. And I always write some message or lesson on the blackboard that I change daily.

MJ: But what were some of the things you came up with just for Pace?

SC: Whenever we were stuck trying to explain something to Pace, we always resorted to a visual support of some kind, like a picture of the next destination to ease transitions or a task board that showed how many jobs he needed to complete before the next break. If he was having a difficult day, we would try to give him ways to communicate rather than kicking us or having a meltdown. We gave him symbols for "I'm mad" or "I need a break" or "I don't understand."

After about six weeks, during the course of a typical day we could see that one simplified portable schedule board and reward system were all we really needed. (See Appendix for example.) The big poster boards were ignored. Few of us could ever find the right Polaroid when it was needed. Schedules were always changing, and unexpected events were always cropping up. We could never hope to keep up with showing Pace what was going to happen next.

Our greatest strength for consistently motivating and directing Pace lay within the children themselves. They were like one big current, moving him inexorably from place to place.

MJ: We eased up on the demands we were putting on Pace, too. We took the daily schedule cards out of the pockets in the weekly schedule device and only showed him one card a day. This card was kept in his back pack, which went everywhere with him. That way babysitters, therapists, teachers and anyone else involved in Pace's life could have instant access to the plan for each day.

We kept a three-ring binder in his back pack that held school work, notes from therapists, information, instructions or requests that went back and forth between the teachers and us, and his daily report from kindergarten. (See Appendix for example.) With so many people contributing to the communication notebook, it would fill up quickly. We wanted to keep it small (about one inch thick), and light enough for Pace to carry easily, so we made a new one about every six weeks, which coincided nicely with the school's grading periods.

We also cut back on extra-curricular "work" times, only going to the park or playground for fresh air breaks and not trying to do too many language-based field trips or activities that would put stress on Pace to perform during his off hours. We did continue to let him relax with books, videos and computer games because even though these provided plenty of opportunities for him to get obsessively absorbed, we suspected that he was also using them to integrate classroom lessons. Often he would choose a CD-ROM or gravitate to books or videos that dealt with exactly the same subject we knew had been discussed in school that day. He has always been a strongly independent learner, and we wanted to respect his right to "cram" knowledge on his own time and in his own way.

SC: What did all that night time stimulation do to his sleep patterns?

MJ: We did have to deal with that; you're right. On the advice of our private occupational therapist, we revived a brushing protocol that had helped us several times before but that we had recently let slide. This gave him a sensory diet that served to even him out, calm him down, and allow him to rest better. This has become very common I think, and most people working with children on the autism spectrum know how to do this, now.

SC: Yes, we have about three brushes in our gadget drawer at school right now. And we use them on a lot of children; not just the children with special needs, either.

MJ: That makes sense. It's a great regulating device.

Brushing Protocol

Get a surgical scrub brush from your occupational therapist or any surgical supply store. Using the side with the most bristles, brush each limb at least 20 times going down the limb and back up. Brush your child's back, the soles of his feet, and palms of his hand the same way. Count out loud so he can anticipate when you will end.

Joint Compressions

Take hold of one joint at a time by putting hands firmly on either side of the joint. Push hands together sharply, but not roughly, in quick succession about 10 to 20 times. Do this to wrist, ankle, shoulder, elbow, knee and hip joints. You may even push down gently on the head to compress the neck joints.

Always consult your occupational therapist before beginning these protocols.

SC: Remember you had us put the brushing protocol into Pace's Individualized Education Plan (I.E.P.) to make sure he would receive this service at school as well.

MJ: Right. It did seem to help with his flare-ups and noncompliance. Also during that time the school occupational therapist offered to swing Pace on the therapy swing for 15 minutes every day before school. She said all we had to do was arrive that much earlier and she would be glad to do that every day. We were so impressed with her commitment to him. She was doing this out of the kindness of her heart, so we certainly were glad to meet her halfway. I think it did jumpstart him into more of an alert and positive frame of mind, don't you?

SC: No question. And speaking of kind, I'll never forget watching Pace with Suzette in the cafeteria. She practically made it her mission to get him to try new foods and enjoy the things she got him to eat.

MJ: Thanks to her, Pace is a huge fan of the cafeteria now; it may be his favorite part of the day. And the word "yum" has become a permanent fixture in his vocabulary.

SC: Probably the single most challenging demand we put on Pace in kindergarten was to learn the life skill of flexibility. Changes in routine are hard. Rituals feel good.

MJ: And I think you can say that one of the hallmarks of autism is rigidity.

SC: We had to find a way to transition between activities that Pace would buy.

MJ: You used music a lot of times, didn't you?

SC: All the time. I have a stack of LPs (the kids call them "big CDs"). These are old, old records of kindergarten-type songs I have had for years, and I have a record player tucked away in a corner of our group rug near my rocking chair. Whenever I need to calm the children down, wake them up, or get them to prepare for a new activity, I put on a record and we sing and dance our way to the next step.

MJ: I used to love to come at the start of your day when you would play that cheerful, time-to-get-up-and-go song.

SC: "It's a Beautiful Day," it's called.

MJ: You'd get them ready for lunch with a count-down song, and send them home with something that re-teaches some lesson of the day like numbers, letters, or colors.

SC: But again, this is not something I created for Pace. This is a device I have used with all children for years. It's just that it worked very well with him, too, because he loved music so much, and it thrilled him to be in the midst of a bunch of singing, dancing children.

MJ: I was amazed to see Pace so willing to stand up with 24 other children and sway to the music as they all jumped, wiggled, and sang at the top of their lungs. Your classroom aide used to stand behind him and take both his hands in hers and make him go through the motions of the song. It didn't look like he was resisting her. Once I eased around the perimeter so I could get to where I could see his face. There was that dimple and the lopsided grin. And everyone seemed so happy.

SC: Oh, they fought to be his "buddy!" This child would model typical things we would do in a day, like putting mail in the mailbox, lunch money in the money drawer, backpack in the cubby, sign-in with their name, and vote on a book to be read at story time. They would show him how to prepare for lunch by putting work away, washing hands, getting lunch money, and lining up. The child would demonstrate the proper way to stay in line, with hands behind the back in a "ducktail," as the class moved around the school.

MJ: Seemed like the girls were always the first to raise their hands to be Pace's "buddy." He's like a big doll to them. They like to take his hand, lead him around, make him imitate things they say, pet him, do things for him, and generally put him under their full control. Pace puts up with this far better from girls than from boys.

SC: Yes, but we don't like to encourage that. It's important for everyone to treat Pace like a boy — in an age-appropriate manner. We used to have to really get after the aides who wanted to coddle him and hold him on their laps. It's not good to treat a child like a baby if he's five years old.

MJ: Oh, I know. It's funny, though. The boys were less patient with Pace. They like structured games with rules, they tend to be more loud and rambunctious, and their nurturing skills are often not as well developed.

SC: One of the most wonderful things I ever saw was one day when the children were singing a song that required the boys to "go in" to the circle at one point, and the girls to "go in" at another, and Pace stepped in when the girls were supposed to go. Manny, one of Pace's best friends, pulled Pace back and said, "Yo, Pace, girls go in, man!" It was so cute, and he really cared that Pace do the right thing.

MJ: Isn't it funny how they all had different opinions of Pace and ways of dealing with him? Some of the children thought Pace was unformed, like a baby. Some were intimidated by his reading skill and thought he was incredibly smart. Some were afraid of his outbursts and wouldn't go near him. Some resented all the attention he got and didn't see why he was so special. Another whole group just loved him, fought to be near him, and celebrated every small academic or social success he gained as though it was their own personal victory.

SC: But I think a lot of that kind of support you are talking about was made possible by the constant presence of an aide.

MJ: There was always someone right there to model the correct way to deal with Pace. There were all your teacher's assistants, occupational and speech therapists, and even the special education case manager herself on some especially rough days.

SC: We tried to get everyone to prompt only as much as necessary, to foster independence and promote interactions with peers. Many days, this was an uphill battle.

MJ: But the typical peers just naturally fueled a powerful desire to belong.

SC: As Pace initiated more and more interaction, we let that power of the peers take over and just made sure we were providing enough visual support to keep the motion going.

MJ: What do you mean "visual support?"

SC: Our best invention was a board with three Velcro strips. (See example in Appendix.) The top strip had picture symbols of all the work to be completed that day. The second strip was blank so that as each job was done, its picture

could be moved down to the "job done" strip. The third strip contained three reward choices that we knew were highly motivating to Pace.
When all his jobs were moved to the "done" strip, he could choose one of these rewards.

MJ: Oh, right, and that's when you asked me for a menu of rewards for the teachers to give Pace. I think the top ones were popcorn, candy, raisins.

SC: Yes, that's what you told me he liked best, but the weird thing was, when he was offered these things, he would just get mad and bat them out of our hands. We figured that Pace decided these were totally inappropriate rewards for school work. And we thought this because he would only accept academically oriented objects like books, puzzles, or OT-related things.

MJ: Do you remember that we had a big conflict over using aversive reinforcement techniques? I tried to get you to squirt water at him with a spray bottle.

SC: And we wouldn't!

MJ: Well, in my defense, when Pace was exhibiting a lot of self-injurious behavior, as well as hitting/scratching/kicking his private speech and occupational therapists, they resorted to squirting him with a spray bottle. They didn't have to use it much, and it didn't take long to fade his negative behavior, but when I suggested it to the team at school, you wouldn't hear of it.

SC: There was no way we were going to use a spray gun on Pace!

MJ: I had to admire your decision, especially after I saw how effective it had been in extinguishing Pace's horrible behavior in the clinical setting, and realized you just were not going to avail yourselves of that option.

SC: We figured we could bring him around another way.

Perceptions, Perseverance, and Practical Answers

The teacher's perspective

We thought we could improve Pace's work-schedule board by putting in some "break" cards at intervals within the task-card line. This meant he could choose a sensory activity — like jumping on the mini trampoline, getting in the ball bag or swinging on the OT swing — whenever he got to a "break." He loved these choices, and they helped to keep him calm.

In those days even a short burst of work was exhausting for Pace and might involve many moments of tantrums and noncompliance on his part and redirection or cajoling on our part. If he knew a reward was coming, we usually got more out of him. A big early breakthrough happened one day as Pace was resisting a group activity and starting to tantrum. He suddenly rushed over to his schedule, got a "break" card, and gave it to his aide. This was one of his first real communications toward us, and it made us very happy.

The parents' view

It was so hard to know what he was thinking and how hard we could push him. Everyone was dying to know how to reach Pace and make him part of the group. I spent a lot of time working with all the other children in the room so I could get some kind of idea of what "normal" was. It was staggering how different the kids all were! I was stunned again and again to witness what I considered to be a totally successful five or six-year-old struggle mightily with something that came easily to my own child; like counting in numerical order, reciting the alphabet, reading. Of course, most of the children were way ahead of him in the more abstract ideas like today, tomorrow, and yesterday.

I thought, surely they were more advanced socially. But I watched children develop phobias about the lunchroom, get their feelings hurt over not being chosen to do something like erase the blackboard, suffer intense embarrassment if they gave a "wrong" answer. I saw kids jockey for position, demand attention, make bad choices, lie, be mean, act lazy, and try to get out of doing work.

Then I looked at Pace — quiet, studious, unconcerned Pace. He never vied for the limelight. That was a deficit. His disorder made him completely uninterested in shared attention. He liked to learn at the computer with headphones on. He liked to eat quietly and read books by himself and was totally happy to spend the entire recess sifting mulch through his fingers, swinging alone, or walking the perimeter. How long would it be before the children tired of his lack of play skills and limited repertoire of responses? When might they give up and move on to a more satisfying project? It just seemed like Pace would always be the odd man out.

The teacher's perspective

I'll never forget the day that we had a lunchtime birthday party for a child, and the child's mother brought chicken nuggets for all the children to eat as a special treat before the cake. Pace had never wanted to participate in birthday celebrations before. They were often too chaotic, and he was always clearly disturbed by the noise and break in routine. He never ate donuts or treats or anything that other parents brought to give to the kids.

So as the chicken nuggets were served, a group of us stood to the side and discussed who would go with Pace to the regular lunch room so he could get something to eat in a more regular setting. One of us volunteered to go with him and the rest turned back to the party in progress. Lo and behold, there was Pace, calmly sitting in the middle of all the other children, completely at ease, wolfing down chicken nuggets as fast as anyone.

There was no question that Pace could be part of that group. He did belong. He was just like everyone else, only more so! By the end of the year, Pace was adhering to my rules, earning Skittles for good behavior, and responding to my famous "look" that I give every child to get them to do the right thing.

He could read. He was starting to be able to write. He knew his letters and numbers. Most of our Work Jobs were a breeze for him. I feel quite sure that when he graduated from kindergarten, he knew basically the same as or more than any child in the room.

What the other children felt

I liked Pace. He's a really good guy! He talked by the way he acts. Each time he was kicking we knew by the way he was acting that he was scared or mad and when he was acting ok we knew that he was alright and that he was having a good time right then.

Jack R.

I liked him when I first met him.

Ray B.

When I got to know him, it turned out pretty good. I spent a lot of time with him in the classroom and I got to like him. He really surprised me how he didn't whine and he didn't feel sorry for himself, and that's what I liked about him.

Morgan T.

One time he said, "Hello," and he almost said my name.

Manny R.

Pace goes like this (drums lips with fingers) when he's happy, and I like that.

Ray B.

Whenever he hurt me or hurt one of my friends, I thought that he was kinda mean, but my Mom told me he had this disease and then I thought "Poop! I totally messed up!"

Jack R.

When he kicked my leg he made me angry.

Ray B.

He scared me when he hit me.

John T.

And when he kicked me.

Manny R.

But he was frustrated.

John T.

Because he couldn't talk.

Manny R.

Discussion
talk
talk

I was proud of myself for playing with Pace and hugging him and he really loved to give me a high five. I was proud of myself for stopping worrying and leaving all that stuff behind me and saying "I can do this" and really playing with Pace.

Morgan T.

I was proud of trying to teach Pace how to talk.

Jack R.

When he wanted to make what I was making, I would show him how.

Macy M.

What the other children's parents thought

Pace was a master with computer games.

MT

I was impressed with how Pace followed directions from Mrs. Hodge, and he tried so hard.

JH

Pace did a great job trying to communicate with peers and teachers. I realized Pace was frustrated at times when no one seemed to understand his needs.

SM

One of the best things I ever saw Pace do was let other children hold his hand and "hold back." He must be a loving child.

LC

It was so cool when Pace decorated his flower pot for his Mother's Day gift. I could tell that he knew that his Mother would love it and be proud.

DM

His reading! It was great!

MB

I felt awkward. I was afraid to interact with him for fear of upsetting him. When he was upset, he seemed hard to control.

SB

Sometimes my daughter would explain to me that Pace didn't like to talk and that he would sometimes kick her, but she said "That's Okay, Mama, he can't help it."

DM

My daughter came home once and told me that Pace had smiled at her.

HM

My son enjoyed Pace and he commented on how he liked it when he laughed.

MB

I loved seeing Pace sing and participate in the morning songs, etc. I loved seeing Pace smile. What a great smile! I knew Pace understood everything I was saying to him — especially when we made eye contact.

SM

My son gave no indication all year long that there was anything different about Pace. I think in his eyes Pace was just one of the kids in his class and he accepted him.

AS

My dear friend sent my daughter a book on Las Vegas and when she took it to school Pace loved it. He looked at it every chance he got. That made my daughter proud that Pace was interested in something that she had.

DM

I'm amazed and a little sad that as much as I was in and out of that classroom last year, I never had any real one-on-one time with Pace to see any unusual behaviors (either good or bad) that stick out in my mind. I just considered Pace a part of the student body of the kindergarten class and never noticed anything that stood out — one way or the other. My son would occasionally report on an incident when Pace would become agitated and act out physically with kicking, etc., but I never witnessed this. I do remember feeling such joy for Pace at his birthday party on the train while watching him open his presents. Even though his verbal attempts at "thank you" were not always successful, his face showed such joy and appreciation and delight at his gifts — especially the books!

BR

I praise the students, parents and faculty for having such patience and tender hearts toward Pace.

PR

What the school professionals saw

I learned so much from being around Pace. I sincerely appreciated the opportunity to work with him. Some of the lessons I learned from Pace were: never assume anything, always keep an open mind, and behavior is communication.

Speech Therapist

I had to think beyond the academic goals to include behavior strategies to get to the goals.

Occupational Therapist

Once Pace learned the rules or directions he did well until someone broke the routine. He showed me the importance of keeping to routine.

Special Education Case Manager

He required one-on-one and his behavior would scare me.

Teacher's Assistant

I teach social skills and this is almost impossible for a child like Pace.

Guidance Instructor

Sometimes, all I could do was pray.

Teacher's Aide

Pace taught me to increase my patience and tolerance, to make needed changes quickly, to be persistent, and that I'm more stubborn than he is!

Special Education Case Manager

He knows I want him to use words, and I will wait just as long as needed until he does use words.

Teacher's Assistant

I always say "hello" to Pace when I see him in the hallways and he usually does not respond. My best moment was the first time he said "hello" back to me, and used my name.

Physical Education Teacher

I enjoyed the way the other students worked with him and that he brought out the good in the other kids.

Music Teacher

I was deeply moved by the reaction of Pace's schoolmates toward him. They loved him, and I felt both he and they greatly benefited by being together. He was placed in a classroom where he was well received by teacher and students alike.

Speech Therapist

I had many "best moments" when I knew I had reached him and could see how bright he is and how easily he learns new skills.

Special Education Case Manager

My goal has been to work *with* Pace by putting him in social situations and more one-on-one interactions, but I was always careful to be right there with him providing the tools to be successful.

Speech Therapist

Never give up. You may not see progress or feel like you've made any. Just take a moment, step back, and take a breath. Now see all the progress. Even the tiniest bit is grand!

Teacher's Assistant

I think that if an educator ever feels that he or she hasn't learned something new by experiencing the individual differences of a child, something is very wrong.

Speech Therapist

How do we encourage the least verbal child in the class to find his "voice" and become a fully participating member of the group?

Over the long term, we want this child to talk more, to tolerate more, to socialize more. These are crucial goals covering extensive time periods. To get these goals, we must look for small changes

Gradually Increase Flexibility and Communication

The title of this chapter, "Finding a Way to Work Beyond Words," indicates that we are modifying our practices more than we are changing the child. Of course, the primary goal is to teach the child to communicate and to be more flexible. Over the long term, we want this child to talk more, to tolerate more, to socialize more. These are crucial goals covering extensive time periods. To get these goals, we must look for small changes. We must help the child improve only gradually. Change and learning are slow, sequential processes. We must keep in mind the fact that our goals are long-term and that progress will be in a step-by-step fashion.

The Relationship Between Frustration and Learning

All learning involves frustration. We want to get it right. As we make gradual progress, moderate amounts of frustration will help motivate us to persist.

As we all do when learning, the child with special needs will experience frustration with our efforts to help him or her learn flexibility and communication skills. All learning involves frustration. We want to get it right. As we make gradual progress, moderate amounts of frustration will help motivate us to persist. Think about learning to read or learning to play a musical instrument. As you start, you will experience frustration with errors, with a lack of perfection. Frustration, in moderation, motivates us to persist.

Although moderate levels of stress can facilitate learning, higher levels of frustration will interfere with learning. This has been proven repeatedly in research on learning and frustration. An absence of frustration does not promote learning. Extreme frustration leads to overload and task abandonment. Moderate frustration leads us to push onward.

As children make progress in learning, they may show moderate amounts of frustration. If frustration is absent, learning is likely to be slower. If the frustration is extreme, it will interfere with sleep, appetite, mood, and social interactions. However, the presence of increased frustration is not necessarily a bad sign. It is likely to coincide with increased learning.

In the previous segment you read about the teacher's and parent's concern about the child's frustration level. They struggled to try to contain the frustration. It was hard to tell if the progress seen was worth the frustration expressed.

Working with and through Frustration

Watch the child's frustration level closely. Moderate levels of frustration are optimal. Try to support the child, but do not reduce demands for learning. Instead, keep the child involved in preferred activities. Stick to a predictable schedule. Use sensory breaks after periods of learning and frustration. Continue your efforts to nurture the child in ways he or she prefers.

If frustration is extreme and persistent, you may have to reduce learning demands. Because many children with autism take up to two weeks to adjust to a new change, be sure to go at least that long before reducing educational demands. If the high frustration level lasts longer than two weeks, then have a team problem-solving discussion. Look for ways to minimize sensory demands. Try to eliminate one stressful activity at school and one at home. Maximize the child's time with preferred activities. Avoid unnecessary changes during periods of high frustration.

Stick to a predictable schedule. Use sensory breaks after periods of learning and frustration. Continue your efforts to nurture the child in ways he or she prefers.

It is a serious mistake to try to change the child more than the setting. Frustration will increase.

Imagine being in a near collision while driving on the expressway. You may react by trembling, feeling weak in the stomach, and being unfocused in thinking. Similarly, children with autism typically do not modulate well.

Note that most of these ideas involve changing the environment. To help the child change, you must change the setting significantly. It is a serious mistake to try to change the child more than the setting. Frustration will increase. Remember from Chapter Three: change the setting more than the child. This will help decrease frustration to a level where the child can learn effectively.

Emotional Modulation of the Child

Closely related to frustration is the concept of modulation. We all work to keep our emotional energy at an optimal level. Occasionally, we fail to modulate this energy. Our emotions shoot up too fast, too far, and for too long. Imagine being in a near collision while driving on the expressway. You may react by trembling, feeling weak in the stomach, and being unfocused in thinking. Similarly, children with autism typically do not modulate well. They may be lethargic at times. They are more commonly overly active. They often lose control of emotional energy and fail to modulate.

Ideally, you will push the child almost to the breaking point, then you will back off so the child can modulate.

Sensory integration activities help a child modulate. Work with an occupational therapist to find the things that work with your child and use these strategies on a regular basis. Some suggestions include a brushing protocol with a surgical scrub brush, deep pressure, joint compression, water play, use of a weighted vest or hand toys. It is not unusual for a child to have trials of any number of the above options until the correct sensory "diet" is achieved. Many techniques employed by occupational therapists may at first seem mysterious or strange. Try to keep an open mind and allow your OT to rehearse and explain them to you until you and your child are comfortable.

Modulation is also promoted by watching the child's energy level carefully so you can intervene before the child falls apart. Ideally, you will push the child almost to the breaking point, then you will back off so the child can modulate. Intermingle preferred and non-preferred activities. Avoid sensations that lead to the highest stress. Alternate language activities with nonverbal activities. Use individualized rewards frequently. Children should receive at least 70% positive feedback and less than 30% negative feedback.

Attend to Emotional Modulation in the Caregivers

Just like the child, caregivers will often experience increased frustration. Pay attention to your own levels and work to modulate them. As with the child, alternate stressful and relaxing activities. Maintain your social supports. Keep at least a little fun in your life. Return to Chapter One and read the comments about attending to yourself. You cannot be effective in learning and teaching unless you modulate your frustration!

As with the child, alternate stressful and relaxing activities. Maintain your social supports. Keep at least a little fun in your life.

"When anyone is absent, I want everyone to miss the person who is not there. I want it to matter."

Sherry Corden

Chapter Five

The Social Maze: Learning to Become a Member of the Community

Pace and friend, Manny R., waiting to perform at May Day festivities.

Parent/teacher dialogue

Mary Johnson: I knew he was going to stick out. I knew the children would notice him far more than a lot of the others in the class because of his unusual behavior, his inarticulate speech, and the fact that he was always accompanied by an adult — someone who would always be right there, guiding him on good days and restraining him on difficult ones. I knew they would be very aware of this different child in their midst, but I wasn't prepared for the fact that they would really grow to care for this child and that he would come to stick out in a positive way.

Sherry Corden: The book that you put together to introduce Pace at the beginning of the year gave him a lot of notoriety.(See reprint of this book in the Appendix.) It made him famous. Intriguing. The book was mostly pictures, written on a kindergarten level, so the children could easily read it themselves, and it allowed them to learn far more about Pace than they knew about each other. That was powerful.

MJ: The thing that struck us right away was the intimacy of kindergarten. It's such a soup. These kids are thrown together every day. They get stirred around, mixed and matched, in large groups and small groups, paired off, lined up, sent out to the playground, made to sit still in a quiet circle in the library, jostle each other in the cubby area packing or unpacking, squeezed on a school bus, or bunched on a bench in the cafeteria. The closeness and the noise never stops. It made us wonder, how is our child, with all his sensory issues and communication difficulties, going to cope?

SC: Don't worry, we thought of that, too. We put several escape hatches into the classroom, like a bean-bag chair in a quiet corner near a window, a box of sensory hand toys near his spot on the group rug. There was a desk just outside the room in the hall. This was normally used as a quiet place to test individual children, but it came in handy when Pace was having trouble dealing with the classroom and needed a place to retreat. The bookshelf provided a haven, too, and we could always put him at a computer with headphones. But most of the time, Pace was sitting right there with us, interacting at his own comfort level, participating, and enjoying himself.

MJ: It actually shocked us to see the degree to which Pace did tolerate the other children. I'd see them crawling all over him in gym class, on the playground, at the computer, in the library, at lunch. I would hold my breath and brace myself for the fireworks, but what actually happened most of the time was incredible. He would just sit there and smile.

SC: It was a point of pride to help Pace. Just about everyone signed on to the concept of promoting Pace's success. If he responded to a question even with a one-syllable answer, they would clap. If he stood up or sat down when he was supposed to, they cheered. One day, when this pretty much nonverbal child read his own name on a cue card out loud, they were astounded. Then, I suddenly had the idea to show him all the children's names on cue cards, and he read and recited each and every one of them in a firm, clear, voice. That blew their minds.

MJ: But did you notice how clear he was about his feelings toward the other children? It was almost a visceral response. He just didn't like some kids and adults. We always wondered if it was their tone of voice, the way they smelled, the energy they gave off, or something more blatant. Maybe the people he didn't care for had said something cruel to Pace, teased him, ignored him, talked "down" to him, like he was a baby just because he couldn't speak like typical children of his age.

SC: Sure, and many times I've seen children grab his hands in spontaneous joy or to get him to do something with them, and I'd think "oh, oh, he's going to blow," but there would be that dimple!

MJ: Did you ever notice times when a child would take his hand, check to see your reaction or my reaction, and lead him to something with great ceremony, as though they were doing Pace this big favor and they wanted us to notice?

SC: Oh, yes. And that would be the time Pace would swat at the other child and make an ugly noise as if to say "Get out of my face, I can do it myself!"

MJ: Yes, he doesn't like to be patronized.

SC: Do any of us?

MJ: No. Sure don't.

SC: Some days Pace would be in a "mood," and we'd wonder what had set him off.

MJ: I honestly think he could pick up on the "vibes" around him. If one of his teachers or aides was particularly grumpy or upset or sad, he seemed to know. I think it made him feel insecure when people he was counting on were "off their game." And feelings of insecurity usually made him not want to do anything.

SC: One thing he did that really surprised us was that if one of the adults around him was feeling bad about something, Pace would often give them a hug or stroke their hair or hand. He seemed to want to comfort people who were in distress. But it was usually an adult. Oddly enough, I rarely noticed him initiate a caring motion toward a child; though many demonstrated caring toward him.

MJ: I think he knew which side his bread was buttered on!

SC: Another way he showed that he wanted to be just like everyone else was the way he respected doing the little jobs we give the kindergarteners. If he was line leader, weather person, table cleaner, or whatever, you had to let him do his job when it was time. You could never skip over him. And he took great pride in fulfilling his duties. For instance, he was normally fairly pokey, always dragging his feet and slowing down to read everything that was hung on the walls and bulletin boards throughout the school. But when it was his turn to be the line leader, he took it seriously and never stopped or dawdled on those days!

MJ: I was sure that Pace would enjoy the tasks you give the children to help them learn responsibility and independence. That seemed well within his reach. He loves doing helpful things at home like sorting the recycling, putting dishes in the dishwasher, taking the dirty clothes to the laundry room. However, I was very concerned about how he would react to big, unforeseen events like fire drills and other sudden, unexpected breaks in routine. I wondered if you would be able to get him out of the building, if the noise would scare him, if he'd ever understand what a person has to do in emergencies.

SC: He was fine. In fact, he tolerated the big interruptions far better than he dealt with the little annoying changes that take place every day, all day long. I think when something seems really important and earth-shattering, it is an obvious good choice to go the way everyone else is going — go with the flow. A big group of your peers all obeying the same command and moving in the same direction is a powerful motivator.

Pace takes his turn while bowling with a friend.

MJ: Around the middle of the year, as I saw Pace become more and more comfortable in the classroom, I began to want more. I wanted him to have friends — real friends — and play dates, and go to parties, and invite people over to play with him.

SC: Lots of parents asked me if I thought Pace would or could come over and play with their child. And then they would say "Of course, Mary would have to come, too."

MJ: Nervously, right?

SC: Well, yes.

MJ: I knew that many of the other parents were unsure about asking Pace to their children's birthday parties, especially if they were planning to have the event at a noisy and chaotic place. He was not comfortable in situations like that, and he sure wasn't going to socialize, eat the refreshments, or play the games. It was good that they asked, though. It's horrible to be left out, and we were grateful they were nice enough to ask, even if we usually said "no, thanks."

SC: I'm glad they did include you. We told everyone at the beginning of the year that if anyone had a birthday party outside of school and invited one child from the class they had to invite everyone from the class.

MJ: Oh, yes, and they did. Most parents really made a point of telling us how much their child talked about Pace and liked Pace. And we tried to create social occasions for the kids who got along with Pace by inviting them on mini field trips with us. We took them to the zoo, a bowling alley, the park, ice skating — anywhere they could have fun together without necessarily talking. It gave the other child and Pace a chance to laugh and enjoy each other in a totally different context and to experience success with completely different activities than the ones they typically did at school.

Pace and John T. share the action of a video game during their bowling adventure.

SC: Right. You are really something if you get invited home with someone else, or they take you somewhere. This kind of activity builds relationships and makes them public. It gave Pace an opportunity to host a fun time and share familiar parts of the world he enjoys with his new friends.

MJ: In a year full of triumphs, there were also plenty of painful moments. I guess the thing that made me feel the absolute worst was the day towards the end of the year when we had class pictures taken. Pace decided that he was not going to go into the gym where the photographer was set up, not under any circumstance, no way, no how. For months, he had been going peacefully with his classmates to every place within the school — to lunch, to the playground, and even to fire drills — without a fuss. But this day, this time, he was not going to go into the gym to get that picture taken.

SC: Believe me, we tried everything. He seemed terrified of going in there. It was a shock to us because he had been so compliant about so many things by that time.

MJ: It never occurred to me he wouldn't go. We hadn't had any trouble like that for a long, long time. I didn't think to go to school with him that day and make sure that he got his picture taken with the group. I didn't realize it was going to be such a problem. If I'd only known, I would have been there in a heartbeat. It meant everything to me for him to be a member of that class

SC: Well, it didn't happen. We couldn't get him in there, and he was left out of the picture.

MJ: Yeah, that hurt. It was so symbolic. The whole point was to include this child. To have him left out of the picture, excluded from the very photo that would prove he had been part of that class, was hard for us to take.

SC: I know. It certainly wasn't our wish. I think everyone was sad over it.

· ·

What the other parents thought

My son didn't know what to think of the "fits" Pace would have when he got agitated or scared. I remember him telling me about them at the beginning of the year. I think he was baffled at how to be Pace's friend, which he knew was important — how to play with him, hang out with him without triggering something that would upset Pace. As the year progressed, my son and the rest of the class (it seems) were becoming more and more comfortable with Pace through good moments and bad. He was a class member and treated as such. By the end of the school year, my son and the rest of the class just completely loved and accepted Pace as Pace! My son would report Pace's accomplishments, and when I was in the classroom during times of achievement for Pace, the whole class would celebrate with him.

BR

In the first few days of school, my son came home and told me that Pace was smart, because he could read, but that he didn't say much. He said that he loved books and the bean-bag chair. He was a little concerned about getting hit, but I assured him that Pace would never direct it at him. He came home from school one day and said that Pace had picked him to go to a special work session with him. He was proud and felt very special and showed me his little toy he got for working with Pace. By the end of the year Pace was a special friend from Mrs. Corden's kindergarten class.

DM

My son likes Pace and would always tell me "Pace is so smart, Mommy. He reads!"

SM

I love that my son enjoys Pace and never thinks that he is any different from himself. He is impressed with Pace's reading, and I know that he attempts conversations with Pace daily.

MB

My son gave no indication all year long that there was anything different about Pace. I think in his eyes Pace was just one of the kids in his class and he accepted him.

AS

All children — given a loving, safe environment — will be accepting of and loving to each other. They need to have that modeled and expected in the classroom. What a gift to these children to be loved, respected and accepted for who they are. Children follow our lead, and if we accept them they will accept each other.

DM

My son didn't really think of him as "special" (different), though he was excited whenever Pace showed attention to him and joined him in some play time.

LC

I told my son that Pace was very smart and ready for kindergarten just like he was but that he would not use words out loud much. I told him that this did not mean he could not be talked to. I encouraged him to talk to Pace and tell him things, even ask questions, and never be scared of him.

DM

We were very fond and protective of Pace.

MT

On a field trip, I saw him move over to share his seat with someone who didn't have one.

SB

My son wanted Pace invited to his skating party. He asked where he was when he was not there. I think he really wanted to be with him in another setting besides school.

DM

My son really cared for him and wanted him to come over. I knew, though, that I couldn't take care of him alone.

LC

I felt that if he needed some kind of special attention I would not know how to handle the situation.

PR

My daughter still napped most days so we only had a few girl classmates over the whole year. Her birthday party was mostly girls. I didn't really think about having Pace over, but if my daughter had wanted to, I would have set it up.

CG

I would love the opportunity to have Pace over to play. I would certainly need detailed instruction from Mary on how to interpret Pace's needs and desires.

BR

We did not have any parties during the school year. My daughter's birthday is in June. She did go to Pace's birthday party, though, and she had a great time. She sat with Pace for awhile and wished him a happy birthday. He was very quiet and that was O.K.

JH

What the school staff and professionals said

Question: How do you think you improved Pace's experience at Rocky Hill?

By accepting him for himself and supporting others who work with him so we could share ideas to increase his success.

Occupational Therapist

Coordinating his needed services to maximize his success.

Principal

Nurturing and love.

Teacher's Assistant

The friendship that Pace and I have acquired — the "mother/son" connection.

Teachers' Assistant

By having the same expectations for him in terms of following class rules.

Music Teacher

Just by exposing him to another face; a different person who is willing to accept Pace for who he is and treat him no differently than I would any other child.

School Nurse

I do not have any contact with him as I work at night.

Custodian

I do not have much contact with Pace. When he comes into the office it is usually to leave for outside therapy or go home early. He seems to be a delight when he is here, but he is always supervised.

Administrative Assistant

I always have Pace respond to others and many times try to get him to speak first. He knows I expect him to use words, and I'll wait just as long as needed until he does!

Teachers' Assistant

I think development of the S.M.A.R.T. (Stimulating Maturity through Accelerated Readiness Training) gym has helped Pace developmentally. Plus, my focus in physical education is on eye-hand coordination with multi-task participation, and Pace has adjusted very well.

Physical Education Instructor

I would like to feel that my emphasis on spontaneous communication helped to make Pace's school experience better for him and for the staff. I also feel that my input on ways to increase Pace's receptive language was also beneficial. I was willing to collaborate with all the professionals working with Pace in order to better meet his communication needs.

Speech Therapist

I don't think I did improve Pace's experience. Only those who worked with him deserve the credit. I have learned just by being around him.

School Psychologist

He almost never talks. He melts down all the time. He hits. How is he ever going to make friends?

Peer Perceptions, Fears, and Realities

The peers show pride in their friendship with Pace and their ability to be with him, help him and learn from him. As is often true in life, the fear of judgment and rejection may be unfounded. The peers will tend to want to be with your child.

Whether our children have disabilities or not, we all wonder how they will be received by their peers. We want them to be accepted and liked. When our children have extra challenges, we may come to fear the peers and their ability to reject those who are different.

However, the fear of rejection by peers is often unfounded. Notice how the peers look at Pace with an open mind, without bias and negative expectations. Maybe this acceptance is based on ignorance or naiveté. Maybe it's based on a lack of experience. More likely, it is based on a lack of preconceived notions.

Pace did stick out, but not as expected. He stuck out in a positive way. He was a unique child with enviable strengths. The peers show pride in their friendship with Pace and their ability to be with him, help him and learn from him. As is often true in life, the fear of judgment and rejection may be unfounded. The peers will tend to want to be with your child.

The Sensory Challenge of Social Interaction

However, you must also realize that social interaction is sensory. Children, more than adults, move, yell, cry, whisper, squeal, touch, and emit odors, good and bad. It is important to make sure these sensations do not drive the child away from peers.

Sometimes simple exposures teach a child that the sensations are not so bad. Other times controlled exposure is needed.

Peer-Mediated Intervention

One of the best ways to control exposure and to build social interest is to train the peers to be good playmates. Peer-mediated intervention has been shown to be an effective component of social skills training. This approach focuses on the peers, not the target child. Peers are taught to control the "commotion" they bring to interaction. They are taught to persist in interaction. They are taught to interact quietly, consistently, and safely.

For more information on peer-mediated intervention, see the article by C.A. Utley and S.L. Mortweet, "Peer-mediated Instruction and Interventions," found in Volume 29 of the magazine, *Focus on Exceptional Children*.

> **Peers are taught to control the "commotion" they bring to interaction. They are taught to persist in interaction. They are taught to interact quietly, consistently, and safely.**

Sensory Escape Hatches

No matter how we plan, we cannot prevent sensory overload. We have all experienced it, but the child with autism has the same experience magnified 100 times. To deal with this, the child must have safe and calming sensory areas in the classroom. This is an essential component of an inclusion plan. What calms the child? What sensory activities help him modulate? How can we incorporate these into the classroom?

A sensory haven will reduce stimulation by blocking extraneous visual, auditory, and tactile stimulation and by providing calming stimulation. Barriers (dividers, curtains) block sight and sound. Space protects the child from the sensory stimulation of peers. Bean-bag chairs and weighted blankets provide deep

> **The child must have safe and calming sensory areas in the classroom. This is an essential component of an inclusion plan.**

muscle pressure. Hand toys give relaxing tactile stimulation. A sensory area provides temporary haven so the child can become calm and begin to cope again.

Play Dates and Nonverbal Games

A good way to teach social interaction is with one-to-one play dates. While a group of children may seem like sensory chaos, one child, in a calm, comfortable setting, provides controlled sensory stimulation.

The sensory area is temporary. The child cannot live in that world all of the time. He or she must learn to cope, especially with people and communication. A good way to teach social interaction is with one-to-one play dates. While a group of children may seem like sensory chaos, one child, in a calm, comfortable setting, provides controlled sensory stimulation. Especially if the peer is socially mature and has some training, the play dates can be very productive. Parents can arrange such play dates with chosen classmates. Hopefully, the skills learned one-to-one with a classmate will follow the classmate back into the classroom.

Even with extra opportunities for social practice, the child with autism is playing in an unfair game: the others all use language well. To level the field, nonverbal games can be used at school and on play dates. On a daily basis, educators should have brief play activities during which talking is not allowed. You can take 15 to 20 minutes from a physical education class or from recess. Use any of the good resources on cooperative, nonverbal play to find games. Two good places to start are *Playing, Laughing and Learning with Children on the Autism Spectrum: a Practical Resource of Play Ideas for Parents and Carers* by Julia Moor, and *Giggle Time — Establishing the Social Connection: a Program to Develop the Communication Skills of Children with Autism* by Susan Aud Sonders. Give the child a chance to interact without having to speak and without the sensory irritation language might provide. By doing so, you are providing opportunities for interaction while adapting to the child's weakness in verbal communication.

Using Strengths to Promote Acceptance

The child's strengths also provide an avenue for having an impact on social interactions. Note how many times Pace's peers talk about how well he reads. They admire him and want to be like him. His strength in reading makes him special in a very good way. Parents and educators may need to do some good public relations work by identifying and advertising a child's strengths. If he is good with numbers, maps, calendars, puzzles, or memorizing, let his peers know about it and experience it. The peers will quickly see this as something of value, and they will be slower to judge the child's challenges.

Perceptions of Peers vs. Adults

Children do not tend to judge, label, and categorize others as much as adults do. They are usually far more accepting of diversity. Let us learn from them! Reread the peers' comments throughout this book. See how open they are and willing to experience and experiment. Children have an innate ability to accept wildly divergent qualities in their peers and overlook differences that you or I might find disconcerting. Peers also have the great power to push specific issues and elicit desired behaviors more readily than teachers and parents can. Watch them in action. The peers will teach you more than I can.

Parents and educators may need to do some good public relations work by identifying and advertising a child's strengths. If he is good with numbers, maps, calendars, puzzles, or memorizing, let his peers know about it and experience it.

"Now, I ask you, how was my child who had never spontaneously said he loved me, much less said even two words about anything to anybody, ever going to say 'Please be my Valentine' to 25 classmates?"

Mary Johnson

Chapter Six

A Break in Routine: Holidays, Disaster Drills and Everyday Upsets

Pace, at 7:00 AM, and not too thrilled about going to the nursing home to celebrate the winter holidays.

Parent/teacher dialogue

Holidays

Sherry Corden: Let's see, there's Rosh Hashanah. Columbus Day. Halloween. Veteran's Day. Thanksgiving. Hanukkah and Christmas. Martin Luther King's Birthday. Valentine's Day. St. Patrick's Day. Easter. Mother's Day. May Day. End-of-the-year Party. In 180 days of school there are an awful lot of celebrations. And parents love to throw a party in my room as many times as I will let them.

Mary Johnson: It was agony for us. Pace struggled with small interruptions to the daily routine. Imagine how he felt every time he had to confront a holiday.

SC: True. There is always a lot going on because we try to get all we can out of every holiday — make it a learning experience, do crafts, expand vocabulary. For instance, at Halloween we talked about different careers and vocations and then made costumes out of large paper grocery sacks that represented the kind of person each child wanted to be when he or she grew up.

MJ: That was a sensory nightmare. First we had to figure out what Pace might want to be since he was not going to tell us. Then we had to decorate the bag, which he didn't want to do. Then Pace was expected to put the bag over his head and walk all around the gym single file with 120 other kindergarten children — all also wearing bags — in front of the whole school in the "Halloween Parade."

SC: A *lot* of the kids find that a little challenging.

MJ: Well, we opted out of that one. It was not going to be possible to get Pace to express an idea about what he would like to be when he grew up, and we sure weren't going to get him to wear a bag over his head.

SC: I know. We understood. You pick your battles.

MJ: Thanksgiving was fun, though. You had the kids outdoors with easels for most of the fall painting great big turkey tails with tempera on brown craft paper. I think they enjoyed that process, and it taught them the color wheel.

SC: Yes, and most of them wore them in the parade we had for Thanksgiving. There was a little resistance to wearing the rubber feet and wattles in some cases, though.

MJ: How about those reindeer sweatshirts you helped the kids make for their trip to the nursing home around Christmas?

SC: Oh, yes. The kids had to dip their hands in brown paint and slap them down on white sweatshirts to make two antlers and then we painted one of their feet and had them step between the hand prints and that made the deer's long face. Then we glued on a red pom-pom for the nose and they all looked so adorable. Pace was willing to do that.

MJ: You must have had him broken in by then. He didn't make it to the nursing home, though. He came down with a cold and had to miss it, sorry to say.

SC: Oh, I don't know. It may have been lucky he couldn't go. There are always certain very strong aromas there. Pace probably wouldn't have tolerated it. And the children's carol singing is usually pretty off-key. And loud.

MJ: How did you handle the issue of cultural diversity in your room during the winter holiday season? How could you explain various traditions to a child who does not even seem aware of his own traditions?

SC: We only talk about cultural diversity if there are children in the room in a given year who do represent different cultures. And then we don't make a big deal of it. I always make sure to have books available that describe different traditions, and sometimes a Mom will come in and do a little show-and-tell.

MJ: Valentine's Day was probably the most frustrating holiday for us. It was so clear that many of the children felt true affection for Pace, and we were pretty sure he was not going to reciprocate in any meaningful way. He wasn't writing then; could hardly hold a pencil. He wasn't talking spontaneously much at all. He rarely gave a hug, never held out a hand, and didn't give much eye contact. I felt sorry for the children who would want to be sweet to him and not get anything back.

SC: Well, I remember you did manage to get him to sign Valentine cards for all the children and it actually was a great exercise in reading and talking for him to deliver each card to each child's bag of Valentines.

MJ: Yes, and I remember taking home his bag and spilling out all the Valentine cards he had received and reading them with him. He didn't pay a lot of attention, and I wasn't able to do it with him for very long, but I think somehow on some level he knew that the children did care for him.

SC: Remember how on St. Patrick's Day we tried to trap leprechauns in home-made traps and look for their pot of gold? You might not know that we had to find someone's baby brother or sister who would be willing to let us put green paint on their feet and make them run all around school after hours the day before St. Patrick's Day. That's how we made "leprechaun" tracks everywhere for the kindergarteners to follow. Now that's a challenge, let me tell you, and just about impossible unless you have a very cooperative child.

MJ : You did something nice for Mother's Day. Remember those flower pots you had the kids decorate with seashells and plant a marigold in?

SC: Pace liked doing that.

MJ: I still have it. Two years later.

SC: That's good, because he was really proud of it.

MJ: And every holiday we had a big class party, with refreshments, games, art activities, and goody bags for the kids to take home. There were always at least seven extra people in the room.

SC: Most Moms and Dads of kindergarteners love to come in and help with special times.

MJ: The food was always great, but different, and at that point Pace was not interested in trying new things. There was so much noise and chaos as the children ate sugary sweets, played games, ran around free, and went into hyper phase. Of course, that's normal, but it was hard for Pace to be around all that without getting agitated.

SC: I know. We tried to make it easier for him. We let him retreat to a separate space, away from the other children. We gave him his refreshments in a quiet corner, but it didn't seem to matter. Most of the time he would not even touch the most tempting treats. We didn't make him join in games. We thought he might like to just watch, but he couldn't even tolerate that. He would lie down and scream or whine or cry. That kind of cast a pall over everything, so we usually just let him go to another, more quiet room in the school.

MJ: It was so hard for me to relate to the other parents at those parties. It was so obvious to all of us that Pace really was different from the other children. He didn't want cookies. He didn't want to play. And no matter how hard we had all worked to try to create a good time, he didn't think any of this was at all fun.

SC: We always saved cupcakes or whatever the refreshments were for him — and the goody bag. We thought that if we sent him home with these things he would still feel included and know on some level that he had been part of the celebration.

MJ: That is true. But the biggest celebration of them all, and the one I never thought he would ever participate in, was the May Day celebration. It's huge. All those kids — 600 in the school, right? All those parents. Must have been over a thousand. The singing, the dancing, the Maypole, the excitement. I remember thinking "how is this kid ever going to put on a costume, come outside, and participate in this chaos?"

SC: It is one of the only things the school does as a whole in which every single child is included. It doesn't matter who you are or what your disability might be. We expect you to be out there with everyone else, singing and dancing. We literally spend the whole year rehearsing and making sure that every child has a role.

MJ: I know. I was shocked the first time I saw it. Some of these kids I had never seen because they spend most of their time in the LRE (Least Restrictive Environment) classroom or where ever. And here they were, as happy and participating as anybody else.

SC: We were afraid the May Day celebration would be hard for Pace. He didn't sing. He wasn't really good at following directions, and his motor ability wasn't up to age level. So that's why we gave him a buddy. Not an aide, not a grownup, but another child a little bit older who would not really stick out from the group and could quietly guide Pace through the motions and keep him on task.

Pace's buddy, Piper Phillips, took her role seriously and helped to make a May Day miracle.

MJ: It worked! Remember, she was the daughter of one of the other kindergarten teachers and very sweet. She held his hand and got him through all the dances, and he followed her like a little pup with a big grin on his face. I cried. I was so sure he would freak out and not even be able to go outside to watch the program, much less perform in it. I didn't bring a video camera. I told my husband not to bother getting off work to come. I didn't invite any of my friends. I barely made it on time to get a good seat myself. Little did I know it would be the high point of his whole kindergarten "career."

· ·

Disaster Drills

MJ: I was really worried about how he would react to big, unforeseen events like fire drills and other sudden, unexpected breaks in routine. I wondered if you would physically be able to get him out of the building, if the noise would scare him, if he'd ever understand what people have to do in emergencies.

SC: He was fine. In fact, he tolerated the big interruptions far better than he dealt with the annoying little changes that take place every day, all day long. I think when something seems really important and earth-shattering it is an obvious good choice to go the way everyone else is going — go with the flow.

MJ: How did you ever get him to go outside and stand quietly in line for as long as he was supposed to? How did you get him to crawl under his desk or crouch against the wall with all the other children? Didn't it seem like a strange request? Didn't he balk?

SC: Most kindergarteners don't understand the reasons behind these drills or the potential danger. And we don't try to explain it. Why scare them when it is only a drill and might never really happen? To them it's just fun. They get to go outside in the fresh air, or crawl under their desks, and it's a big game.

MJ: So there's a feeling of urgency but not of fear.

SC: Right. When we have lock downs I tell them we are "hiding" and we have to close the blinds and close the doors and our principal, Mr. Dent, and the school secretary, Miss Dilworth, are going to be walking down the hall, listening and watching. I tell them it's a contest. If they hear us or catch us hiding we won't win the game, but if we fool them, we will win and all have Skittles. They think that is great fun and Pace picked up on that.

•••

Every Day Upsets

MJ: How about when that van came around for those routine vision tests and hearing tests that are provided by the county? How did you prepare Pace for that?

SC: Social stories really came in handy with those kinds of situations. (See Appendix for examples.) The people who are going to run the tests give you a card with an "E" on it beforehand so you can practice with the children. We hold it up and practice pointing, covering one eye, and calling out the letter. For the hearing test, we talk about wearing headphones and listening and the hand motions that they will want you to make. Pace seemed comfortable with it all after we had run through it a few times.

MJ: We've talked about the picture-taking fiasco in another chapter, but what could we have done to maybe make that event more of a success for Pace?

SC: I've thought about that a lot. I think the key would be to have a social story about how you get your picture taken, describe it all, admit it might not be pleasant, but stress the importance of being a member of the group. It might be good to go to a quiet room and have a practice run, making it all as real as possible. Maybe ask a few typical peers to come along and model the desired behavior. Then you could have rewards for entering peaceably, sitting still, and smiling.

MJ: I used to panic thinking about times you might have to be absent or on professional leave. You were such a strong force in that room and no-one could ever measure up as far as we were concerned. How did you feel about it?

SC: Well, I never like to be away from my kids, and I always try to make sure there will be ample and appropriate coverage whenever I am gone. I prepare the children by telling them why I won't be there. I explain who will be there, and we practice the person's name and write it on the board, and we review our rules and all. I make sure to tell the children when I will be back and then try to keep it simple for the substitute; nothing new, only review and easy lessons and activities. There are some very specific and particular routines that we do every day, like the calendar, and I ask my classroom assistant to perform those duties so the children won't be rattled.

MJ: What about visitors to the classroom? You are the most experienced teacher on your grade level, so it seemed like there were always people observing — other professionals, prospective parents, college students, you name it.

SC: It was common. But it does not bother me to have visitors in the classroom, so it doesn't bother the children. They are so used to Moms helping all the time and they are so focused on what they are doing, I don't think they even know someone else is there half the time. You know, the way I feel, it's my classroom, and it is Pace's classroom, and if something weird happens, it's the visitor's problem, not ours.

MJ: Another area I worried about was what would happen if Pace ever got sick during the day. How would you know what was wrong, since he couldn't tell you, and how would he do with the nurse?

SC: It's pretty obvious what's wrong in a child that young. If they are sick, they're usually exhibiting clear signs and signals. However, because Pace couldn't seem to pinpoint the problem when things were wrong with him, he was a little more difficult to read. After a while, though, we learned he did have some ways of showing us when he wasn't feeling his best.

MJ: What did you see?

SC: He would sometimes act aggressive if he was starting to develop a head cold or ear infections. I think his hearing was affected anytime fluid built up in his head or sinuses and caused him a lot of discomfort.

MJ: We definitely saw that at home.

SC: Sometimes he would get listless and floppy and even fall asleep in the middle of the floor. If we suspected he was coming down with something, he usually was. So we would send him to the nurse with an aide who could interpret for him and get him to cooperate with the examination.

MJ: Would he do that?

SC: Oh, yes. In fact, towards the end of the year if he needed to see the nurse, and the situation didn't seem too bad, I would send a peer with him who was verbal and outgoing and that was a good way to help him start transitioning towards being more independent.

The bottom line through all this is: kindergarteners are all just children, and you can't keep certain things from happening to them — especially unexpected things. You will do your best, you will try to head off all disasters, but something *will* happen, at least once a day. You can count on it. My colleague across the hall, Carol Phillips, had two kids break their arms in one day. Things happen! And it all helps us learn the life skill of flexibility.

He's doing pretty well most of the time. How do we keep him from being thrown by special days and unexpected events?

Regularity. Routine. Repetition.
Regularity. Routine. Repetition.
Regularity. Routine. Repetition.

If the child cannot stand to participate, or even to watch the celebration, what are we teaching about the holiday? Why associate sensory chaos with the special day?

The sensory, communication, and social challenges of autism often lead to strong needs for regularity, routine, and repetition. Holidays and disaster drills are the opposite of regularity, routine, and repetition. Holidays come infrequently and unpredictably, and each one has its own new routines and sensory experiences. They really can present confusing, meaningless "sensory nightmares."

It's O.K. to Opt Out Occasionally

Sometimes the best move is to "opt out," as Mary stated. This may seem like a big deal, avoiding a very special day of celebrations. However, the holiday does not automatically hold interest for the child. Instead, it is a challenging day of sensory chaos. If the child cannot stand to participate, or even to watch the celebration, what are we teaching about the holiday? Why associate sensory chaos with the special day?

Create Alternate Holiday Rituals

When we opt out, we may be able to find quieter, subtler ways to celebrate a holiday. The goal is to create simple shared rituals that might be enjoyable. This may mean careful preparation and repeated explanations. It may mean plans to dress in a specific color and sing and dance with one preferred adult or peer. It may mean a box of cards or decorations without the social stress of giving and receiving things while the room swirls with sound, smell, and movement. A meaningful celebration may mean one specific game or a specially prepared and served helping of a preferred food. It is likely to mean specific and carefully controlled activities that are quiet and low key. It is likely to mean a good deal of participation in the "normal day" routine, with only a brief celebration. Photographs will help, as they can be used year after year to build an understanding of the shared rituals. Social stories will remind and prepare.

Interruptions and Emergencies = Sensory Overload

Fire drills are, by definition, sudden, shrill alarms leading to specific rituals that are performed at unpredictable times. There is a unexpected, loud noise and instant tension and excitement. Children react quickly, and teachers snap important sounding orders. Another alarm means duck under your desk for some unknown and unpredictable reason. Other alarms send kids scurrying around to hide or walking in line to crouch in the hallway. I can't think of a better way to provoke sensory overload in a child who is defensive to sound, movement, and touch.

The goal is to create simple shared rituals that might be enjoyable. This may mean careful preparation and repeated explanations.

Fire drills are, by definition, sudden, shrill alarms leading to specific rituals that are performed at unpredictable times.

Explain. Adapt. Prepare.

Preparation is the key to adaptation. Just as we prepare for the holidays, we should prepare for the disaster drill.

Preparation is the key to adaptation. Just as we prepare for the holidays, we should prepare for the disaster drill. The first few times, take the child outside before the fire alarm sounds. Talk about what is about to happen. List it as a schedule of expectations. Talk the child through the experience. Later you will be able to review for a few minutes before the alarm and then participate as planned. Change the setting to gradually teach the child. Forcing an overwhelming experience will teach little. Planning a sequence of expectations may teach much more.

Shared Experience Makes for True Inclusion.

The sharing of experience is an integral part of intervention. It is a key reason for inclusion, so we will adapt but find ways to participate.

The child is prepared for the variations in routine. These variations are minimal and are carefully controlled. The child is able to experience the sharing of an activity. This sharing of experience wears away at the social isolation of autism. The sharing of experience is an integral part of intervention. It is a key reason for inclusion, so we will adapt but find ways to participate. We will look at the child's preferred activities and how these can be incorporated into a shared experience. We will share the things the child is able to enjoy in the celebration or in the fire drill. Marching together is fun. Singing together is fun. A box of Valentines is fun. Maybe learning together is fun, too.

"I thought Pace was challenging, but once everyone learned what he needed and how to work with him, he wasn't as frustrated, didn't need to fight anymore, and became a delight to work with.

Sandy B.
Occupational Therapist

Chapter Seven

Environmental Issues and Sensory Strategies

Sometimes it only takes a simple solution to screen out unwanted noise.

Parent/teacher dialogue

Sherry Corden: As soon as I met Pace and saw how withdrawn he was, I worried he wouldn't succeed in my class unless I made it my goal to get him right in the middle of everything, right in the midst.

Mary Johnson: And we worried that if he was surrounded on all sides by squirming, curious, noisy children, he would start hitting and never stop until everyone was down.

SC: The more I got to know this child, the more I could see him as an adult in a leather wingback chair in his own well-stocked library, sitting and reading, all alone. That's when I decided I was going to be in his face all the time, making him do things and buy into this concept called kindergarten.

MJ: The biggest barriers to Pace buying into this concept called kindergarten were largely environmental and sensory.

SC: That's why the most helpful thing to me was to have a close relationship with the occupational therapists working in the school and to be able to consult with them on an almost-daily basis. All year long we found ways to minimize distracting elements of our environment and to enhance learning by purposely introducing other sensory devices.

Sound

MJ: I saw the constant barrage of sound you have at school as your biggest sensory challenge. Alarms go off, the intercom rudely interrupts your lessons, the children cough, sneeze, yell, babble, scream, and laugh loudly. There is a continual buzz of noise and energy in the room.

SC: If a sound was annoying or produced anxiety, we did all we could to desensitize any of the children who were disturbed. For instance, when we do the calendar every day, we blow up a balloon that represents "today" and pop the balloon that was "yesterday." Most children do not like the sound of a balloon popping.

MJ: It looked to me like some did.

SC: Most don't. So we make a big deal of letting one of the children take the thumbtack and pop the balloon while the others cover their ears or shut their eyes or do whatever they need to do to cope.

MJ: I don't think Pace ever got used to it.

SC: You're right. He never liked it, but when his turn came he did manage to pop it himself, with hand-over-hand help from his aide.

MJ: How about the cafeteria? How did you ever get him to be so good about going in there?

SC: I don't really know. We thought the cafeteria would be unbearable for him, but it wasn't. I think the orderliness with which they go through the line and the way in which everything is laid out in a very organized manner is pleasing to a child like Pace, and there is all this food that he thinks is wonderful, and the routine is always predictable. I think these good things far outweigh any negative response he might have to the noise. Also there is so *much* noise that it becomes indistinct — kind of like white noise — and maybe that is easier to bear than what happens in the more contained atmosphere of a classroom.

Taste

MJ: Let's talk about the sense of taste for a minute. You know how kindergarten gives a child an endless array of things to eat — and not all of it can be exactly classified as food.

SC: Yes, yes, I know. The whole paste-eating thing.

MJ: Among other things. But, for instance, school lunch is obviously a whole new adventure, offering many strange new tastes and textures.

SC: Yes, and we have to credit Suzette, the aide who went with Pace to lunch every day, with getting him over his aversion to trying new food. She made it her cause to get him to experience lots of different kinds of food. She didn't do hand-over-hand, but she did do mind-over-matter! Every time she introduced a new food to him, she would model eating it with great enthusiasm and make lots of noise about it, like "yummmmmmmm, oooh, yummy. Isn't this gooooood?"

MJ: It worked. He likes a whole bunch of new things now that I never thought I would see him eat.

SC: He got chances to try new things in the classroom, too. Snacks are a daily event, and depending on who is supplying it, we'll have everything from nutritious and familiar treats to ethnic specialties to just plain junk.

MJ: That's true, plus holiday and birthday celebrations give the children a non-stop sugar "high" from all kinds of sweets.

SC: We try not to have too many sugary treats for holidays and birthdays, but life is short and donuts are plentiful.

MJ: I know! It seemed like every time I was in your classroom I saw a box of donuts beside your planning book.

SC: What can I tell you? Kindergarten is hard work. It may be the hardest job these kids will ever have. And everyone does better with rewards. Children love sweets. So do teachers. And Skittles make the world go 'round in my room!

MJ: I know. Then, of course, there's the temptation to munch on markers, chew on crayons and pencils, and eat paste and paper. I suppose that's caused by stress, too?

SC: Some of it is I'm sure. But most children will tell you these things taste good! However, I never saw Pace eat anything that wasn't food. He did — and I hate to mention this, but I have to because a lot of other kindergarteners do it, too — pick his nose and eat it.

MJ: Yuk! Please! We are still working on that!

SC: That's very normal. It's just about impossible to break a child of that habit. Usually it doesn't disappear until the child is interested in attracting the opposite sex.

MJ: So what do you do?

SC: If a child is drawn to eating things he or she shouldn't, usually we do a social story about it and systematically redirect the child every time we catch him or her at it. We also enlist the peers to correct the child, with a calm, clear, short, but kind command. We might say something like "That's yucky! Please use a Kleenex!" And we keep a lot of tissue boxes around the room.

Touch

MJ: What are all the textures and things a child in kindergarten can feel? Mulch on the playground. Beans and sand. A rough carpet. A smooth table.

SC: A classmate's hair. A polyester dress over a slithery slip. A dollop of paint.

MJ: The bristles of a paintbrush. A cool chunk of clay. A soft piece of felt.

SC: Glue on fingers!

MJ: Dried mud in the ridges of a sneaker!

SC: The thrill of running your hand down the entire length of a smooth but bumpy painted cement block hallway! Which is something we discourage, by the way.

MJ: All those textures are so powerful. Some of them make Pace more calm, and some of them completely obliterate his ability to attend to anything other than the immediate sensation at the end of his fingertips.

SC: Yes, it's definitely a big part of our lives in kindergarten. The day I knew I had ceased to be a person and had truly become a "Kindergarten Teacher" was the day one of my students was sitting very close to me in the class circle on the rug and was absent mindedly rubbing his hand up and down my leg to feel the smoothness of my stocking.

MJ: What did you do?

SC: Well, the principal walked in and we had a whole discussion about something or other as this child kept feeling my leg up and down, up and down. Finally, the principal stopped, looked down, and said, "It's okay with me if that kid rubs your leg, but I don't think Mrs. Quirk is going to tolerate that in fifth grade, do you?"

MJ: And you said….

SC: I hadn't even been aware that it was going on! Children are all around me all day, and I hardly ever think about my personal boundaries I had gotten to the point of being far more worried about them getting into my record collection than feeling my leg!

MJ: But what about Pace? How did you handle all of his sensory issues?

SC: It was great that he had those needs. We used them to our full advantage. We gave him a whole box of things he could manipulate and use to calm himself and stay attentive in our group sessions.

MJ: Like what?

SC: Oh, small balloons filled with sand, something called Thera-Putty that we got from the school OT, various items that were scrunchy or textured or rubbery.

MJ: That was good for group sessions, but how did you keep him focused during his individual work times?

SC: We had a special textured and inflated rubber cushion for him to sit on and occasionally used a chair that actually was made out of a big rubber ball set in a frame. He had a slanted surface on which to write, pencils and markers with grips to help with his hand position, and plenty of OT exercises to build web space and distal control.

MJ: Any special tricks for when he got agitated?

SC: When he needed a time out to collect himself we let him go to a bean bag chair in a protected corner of the room that had books and puzzles nearby that we knew he liked.

MJ: Was there a prescribed OT program that you used to help get him ready for the day?

SC: Yes, he often had a short session of swinging in the morning before he started the day, but we found that it was important to make sure that Pace got what we call OT breaks all through the day. That meant either taking him to the OT room to swing in the swing or jump on the trampoline or be given a deep pressure "squish" on the big therapy ball or be put in the "ball bag."

MJ: Explain "ball bag," please.

SC: It's just a huge drawstring polyester bag filled with about 100 small plastic balls. You can get these in bulk at places like Toys R Us. The bag is just a big sack that anybody could sew. You just need to know how to make the channel for the drawstring.

MJ: Or any OT supply catalog would have them, right?

SC: Right, but for a lot more money! Anyway, Pace would climb right into the ball bag and the overall pressure on his muscles would actually have such a relaxing effect that often he would fall asleep right then and there.

MJ: Oh, I need one of those at home.

SC: I'll bet you could make one! Anyway, recess was important, too. Pace really needed that unstructured break and the chance to be outdoors. He looked like he was in heaven if someone pushed him high on the swing and the wind would ruffle his hair.

MJ: I know. At the first preschool he ever went to, the teacher there used to say that when she watched him out on the playground and saw how much he enjoyed every little breeze, she wished she could go to "Pace World" herself for a while.

SC: He does have a heightened awareness of the natural world, that's for sure. He's a very sensual child and I think the sun and breezes and the feel of sand sifting through his fingers is deeply satisfying to him. He's one for noticing the tiny details and variations in texture.

MJ: Yes. He's obsessed with hair and he will be the first one to notice a new hairstyle. He'll be all over it, touching and feeling.

SC: Let's not tell Mrs. Quirk in fifth grade, shall we?

Sight

SC: One big lesson to me was to not overdo the whole picture symbol thing. I started the year putting every possible message up in some kind of picture form for Pace. I had everything we would do that day — every destination, every person he might encounter, every daily routine. He could have cared less.

MJ: He is a visual learner, but sometimes I think too much visual stimulation is confusing to him. He finds it hard to pick out the main event.

SC: It was much more effective to use pictures very sparingly and only to get him from point "A" to point "B." The physical power of the children moving from place to place and doing what they were supposed to be doing — lining up, standing, sitting, washing hands, going to lunch — the overwhelming power of the group just pulled him along and was far more compelling than any pictures.

MJ: The more he saw the other children modeling what he was supposed to do, the less you had to explain.

SC: He just bought into it. And I supported this natural tendency to follow along by providing visual cues for *all* the children to follow. I put different colored tape down on the floor to indicate key traffic patterns in the room.

MJ: Such as?

SC: Like a green line showing the path to take to the drinking fountain and a blue line that went to the place where they got their lunch money.

MJ: That helped them transition from recess to getting a drink of water, to preparing for lunch.

SC: Right. And I have a red tape that shows them where to line up for lunch and so on.

MJ: I get it. That must have given the children a boundary and trained them to walk in a line.

SC: Yes. Which is a pretty unnatural thing when you think about it.

MJ: Because there is not reference, no faces, you are just looking at the back of the child's head in front of you.

SC: Nothing else really cues you what to do.

MJ: So the tapes and the feet outlines you put down really helped.

SC: Yes, and for organizing work and practicing for breaks in routine we relied heavily on picture symbols and social stories to outline what was expected and how Pace should act.

MJ: I know that worked really well and was very comforting to him. I remember how he clutched the picture symbol for "pumpkin patch" in his hand the whole 45 minutes on the bus trip to our field trip to the pumpkin farm at Halloween.

SC: It helped that you had used picture symbols with him for so many years before he got to kindergarten. It made things clear and was something he was used to.

MJ: It didn't help much with his overall tendency to get obsessed with visual stimuli. Have you ever seen him fascinated with something like a speck of dust sifting in a shaft of sunlight?

SC: Yes, right when I'm trying to read a story to the class or explain something important.

Pace, in transit with picture symbol in hand.

MJ: So what were some of the ways you reduced visual stimuli?

SC: One really easy thing I do is to make all the children's tools and supplies the same color.

MJ: How?

SC: I purchase all the same pencils, the same red pencil grips, the same-colored folders that go back and forth from school to home, and identical pencil boxes for the children to use at school.

MJ: That all sounds good.

SC: It really helps the children focus better on the work than the tools to do the work.

MJ: I see. But how do you manage the things you can't control? How do you keep the children from being distracted by visually stimulating things you *have* to have in the room. Like, I've seen Pace obsessively look at your teaching manuals or read the spines of the videos you have stored in your closet.

SC: My way of dealing with that is to put a red paper circle on anything I don't want the children to touch. It's pretty clear to most of them.

MJ: Did it work with Pace?

SC: I had to do a little more with him. He had such a fascination with my records, tapes and CD collection. The trouble is these things are precious tools to me. I use them everyday, and some of them can't be replaced. But Pace wanted to read the labels all the time and study them. So I wrote my name on each one with a bold Sharpie pen and told him they were Mrs. Corden's personal property and he was not to touch any that had my name on them.

MJ: And?

SC: We really didn't have any trouble over it ever again. Except one time. Do you remember?

MJ: I'm not sure. When?

SC: I will never forget this because I thought it was so telling about him. Do you recall how you told me Pace had never acknowledged you as his mother?

MJ: Oh, yes. It used to make me so sad that he had never said "Thank you" to me, or "I love you, Mommy," or even called for me when he was hurt. I used to find him in a dried pool of blood some mornings when I went in to wake him up, and I'd be so upset that he had obviously had a nose bleed and had not called for me in the night when it happened.

SC: So you figured that he didn't even know you as "Mom."

MJ: Kind of.

SC: Well, the day I'm talking about, he proved beyond a shadow of a doubt he knew you were "Mom."

MJ: How?

SC: We had been doing just fine with him respecting my property and leaving my things alone. Then you visited the classroom after not having been there for a while, and the minute you arrived I saw him go straight for the record collection.

MJ: That's right. And you said, "No, sir. Those are Mrs. Corden's records and you are not to touch them," and he backed right off.

SC: But he checked your reaction first. And that was just like any other child. Whenever their Moms come in the room, all of a sudden they misbehave and do all kinds of things they would never do if their Mom was not there. I think they think it'll be O.K. because their Mom will defend them.

MJ: I see what you mean.

SC: That was one of the first times I remember thinking "this child is just like any other child," and I was so glad that he obviously knew very well that you were his mother.

MJ: Speaking of being like the other kids, do you think he was able to read your facial expressions and pick up social cues from common body language as well as the other children?

SC: That's a really good question because it is often said that children with autism can't read those cues. I felt like he did react to my facial expressions. Whenever I gave him the "look," he stopped what he was doing and fell in line as fast as any other child. And appeared just as guilty.

MJ: Good!

SC: I did worry that because Pace was so visually acute, he would have trouble decoding the amount of clutter I have in my room. But the way I break all the kids in is to introduce academic things little by little, putting up math, language and science materials bit by bit. He didn't seem to be bothered or distracted by anything, though.

MJ: Even when the room décor got to be quite busy toward the end of the year?

SC: Even then. I did notice that he seemed to cling to the things that did stay constant, like the calendar, letters and numbers displays, and color charts. It was very unsettling to him if we skipped anything in the daily routine that had to do with any of these big obvious visual aids. He really loved being a kindergartener and wanted to be sure to do everything we were supposed to do.

Smell

MJ: The cafeteria smells. The gymnasium smells. We all know the students' bathrooms smell. There are intense aromas everywhere — the fish bowl, the hamster cage, the cubbies.

SC: The remains of my micro-waved lunch in the trash can.

MJ: The paint, markers, and glue.

SC: And the children themselves certainly have a diverse collection of scents!

MJ: I have no idea why, but Pace did not seem at all bothered by any of the smells.

SC: Some children are, and some aren't. Maybe it's a developmental thing.

MJ: Maybe.

SC: I do know that he can smell a bag of popcorn being popped from a mile away, but that's about all I noticed.

Sometimes our child seems too sensitive and sometimes he just seems oblivious to everything. What can we do to "even him out" so he can get the most out of being in the classroom?

The Pleasure and Pain of Sensation

Our senses bring us pleasure, as with the sound of good music, the smell of coffee brewing, the feel of silk, or the taste of fresh bread. Our senses also bring us discomfort or pain, as with the smell of burning plastic, the shock of a hot iron, or the taste of curdled milk. Sometimes our sensory systems are flooded. This can happen when you're lost in a busy, noisy crowd or when you're overwhelmed listening to conversation when there are multiple loud sources of background noise.

Imagine the pleasure, discomfort, or sensory overload most of us feel as a matter of course magnified ten times, or even a hundred times. This is similar to the sensory world of a child with autism.

Imagine the pleasure, discomfort, or sensory overload most of us feel as a matter of course magnified ten times, or even a hundred times. This is similar to the sensory world of a child with autism.

Sensory Processing as the Basis of Symptoms of Autism

All children with autism have abnormal sensory processing. Senses hurt more. Senses captivate more. With these exaggerated responses to sensations, it is difficult to attach the correct meaning to senses. The sound of a vacuum comes to mean pain. The sight of symmetry captivates to the point where nothing else matters. Sensory overload can lead to complete shutdown or total meltdown.

The sound of a vacuum comes to mean pain. The sight of symmetry captivates to the point where nothing else matters.

Predict the Flashpoints of Sensory Dysfunction

Language is sensory. It is possible that the language and social problems of autism are based on abnormal sensory processing where sensations take on meaning that interferes with learning and socializing.

We all have sensory differences. The sound of fingernails on a blackboard is painful to some but not to others. Different brains react differently to the same sensation. Some of us are very ticklish; others are not ticklish at all. Some of us are sensitive to some odors and gag easily in response to others. Crowds overwhelm some of us. Some of us hate specific textures in clothing, most commonly the tags. Magnify and mix these, and you will have a better understanding of the sensory world of the child with autism.

Control the Environment to Minimize Sensory Triggers

As you work to help the child with autism, you must address these sensory processing issues. When you can, make sensations predictable. A clear routine will help. Consistency will help. Advance warnings can also help. Still, the child with autism will overreact.

Whenever possible, reduce extraneous sensations. Minimize background noise. Work to keep the peers as quiet as possible. Keep the energy level under control as much as you can. Although pictures, charts, mobiles, and manipulatives promote learning in young children, keep these to a minimum if you have a child with autism present. It is sometimes possible to keep this type of visual stimulation restricted to one area of the classroom. Look at the background of the learning field and keep that area free of visual distractions.

It is possible that the language and social problems of autism are based on abnormal sensory processing where sensations take on meaning that interferes with learning and socializing.

As you work to help the child with autism, you must address these sensory processing issues. When you can, make sensations predictable.

Gradually Desensitize the Child

In general, if a child is upset by a sensory event but can calm within five minutes or so, this sensory event should be repeated. If the recovery is over 15 minutes, avoid that sensory event whenever possible.

Although you can minimize some sensory events, fully avoiding noxious sensations will not help and is not possible, so we must gradually expose the child to these, hoping to desensitize him or her. Start with sensations that are annoying, but be brief. In general, if a child is upset by a sensory event but can calm within five minutes or so, this sensory event should be repeated. If the recovery is over 15 minutes, avoid that sensory event whenever possible. A quick recovery is good practice. A long recovery will leave a strong negative memory, and the meaning of the sensation will be associated with this. Provide repeated trials of sensory threats that are followed by a quick recovery.

Use Sensory Preferences to Your Advantage

In addition to controlling the threatening sensations, we must also control the absorbing sensations.

In addition to controlling the threatening sensations, we must also control the absorbing sensations. If a child likes to stare at round objects, falling objects, or dangling objects, then he or she is not attending to the correct meaning and will not learn efficiently. However, you cannot fully outlaw this type of behavior. It can center the child and calm him or her. Instead of working to fully stop absorbing sensory responses, work on periodically interrupting them. As the child is staring, call his name, pull out a preferred object, or give a simple direction (e.g. "Pace, touch your nose"). Persist until the child responds. Once he does, it may be O.K. to let him go back to staring briefly. These types of interruptions help the child gain control of the absorbing sensory responses. He learns to stop and to start, as we all do when we daydream, and then orient to a friend calling our name.

Repetition helps normalize sensory responses. This leads the child to gradually change the meaning attached to sensations. If this works, you will see a quicker change in the language and social symptoms of autism.

Please Note

Sensory integration is a very complex topic. All who help care for the child with autism should become students of sensory processing theory and practice. To do this, find a good occupational therapist who is experienced with sensory integration dysfunction. Look for workshops on this topic. Consider reading the book, *Sensory Integration and the Child* by Jean Ayers. Also look at the book, *The Out-of-Sync Child: Recognizing and Coping with Sensory Integration Dysfunction* by Carol Stock Kranowitz. The more you know about sensory integration, the more effective you will be in your work with autism.

"My advice to the next class that Pace is in? Be nice to him and make friends with him because he is a really sweet guy and he's nice. He may be different but he's still nice."

Morgan T.
Kindergarten classmate

Chapter Eight

Making Friends and Moving On

Pace in a jubilant moment with his everpresent "pod of peers."

An Open Letter to Pace's Next Teacher

Dear Next Teacher,

Here I go offering advice, when at least once a week I say to myself about advice others have given me: "I'm glad I didn't take that piece of advice to heart!" So I offer this letter humbly and without fanfare. Take it for what it is worth; it is only what I have learned based on my perception, and perception is not an exact science.

We all see things differently through the lens of our own assumptions, agendas, prejudices, likes and dislikes, and rarely do any two of us see things exactly alike. In fact, Mary and I started this whole interesting dialogue precisely because we discovered that we both had absolutely different views of our very first meeting the spring before Pace entered kindergarten. This was the meeting in which we, and the whole team, developed his Individualized Education Program (I.E.P.). I later learned that Mary was in a panic because she thought I would not accept Pace and would "kick him out" of my class at the first sign of trouble. And I remember I was in a panic because I dearly wanted this child to succeed in my classroom, and I was afraid I would not be able to figure out enough ways to keep him there. So —

Tip #1: Don't even for a minute consider that what you believe to be a common truth is truth for anyone but you.

Develop a relationship and open up those lines of communication from the very beginning. I know as teachers, we are often discouraged from doing that. The system almost always sets us up as "them" and "us." There are those laws, you know. You might say too much and get us in a fix. Discuss your concerns honestly, try not to assign blame, and touch base frequently. See your self, the other school professionals, and the parents as a team with one focus: the child's welfare.

Tip #2: Teachers and parents come from different places and have different perspectives. They can't help it. Let the teacher be the teacher, and let the parent be the parent.

Sometimes teachers want the parent to be more "teacher like" and have their child in student mode 24 hours a day. It won't happen, because she is his mother. She sees him through a mother's eyes. And even though you, the teacher, may also be a mother to your own children, you are not your student's mother. You may sense that the parent of your student wants you to be a little more nurturing or "mother like." Don't do it. You are the teacher. Behave like the teacher. This is what you are trained to do, and you must take the lead in the child's education. You can certainly collaborate, but never let the parent try to design the academic program. The child will benefit the most if you will both fulfill your own unique roles.

Tip #3: Don't worry about making mistakes. They have all been done before.

There is a very large and very strong net waiting to catch you if you fall. I have landed there many times, and I'm a better teacher for it. Almost all of the individuals who make up the support and special-area staff at Rocky Hill live up to their name and beyond. You are the classroom teacher and the center of the educational universe. You will need support, questions answered, materials adapted, an extra pair of hands or eyes. They will be there if you ask.

Just about every day you will discover an area in which you lack expertise. You are the classroom teacher. You design the basic educational unit. Lean on those who are well-versed in ways to tailor your program to a child's special needs. You can find them in your school, in the larger system, and even on the internet.

So when you need a specialist, ask for one. One will appear. And they will appear with good will because they like to be asked. Everybody likes to exercise their talent and put their training to work. They will not look down on you or put you to shame for needing them. You know typical growth and development patterns. They know all the ways you can help a child with autism have more success through occupational therapy, speech/language intervention, and behavior management techniques. It is the combination of everyone's talents and skills that will benefit the child. If integration is the main goal for a child with autism, then let the integrating begin with all of us who are on the team.

Tip # 4: Remember, a child like Pace is just a little boy.

His I.E.P. meetings may include 10 people or more, all explaining his strengths and weaknesses and deciding upon his goals. In the end you will find that his needs and wants and frustrations are like any other child's — just multiplied times 10.

He wants to be in school. I believe he tolerates some things that are pretty intolerable to him just to make it through the day. If you are truly in charge of your classroom, he will recognize it immediately. Just make sure you are. Be organized. Make visual cues/reminders a part of the classroom. Develop routines. These things are good for everybody.

Tip # 5: But he does take in information differently than other children.

We all want children to look at us when we are speaking, but a child with autism may find it easier to listen better when his back is turned or he is halfway across the room. It may be less distracting for him to take away the visual stimulation so that he may attend to the verbal message. Also, background and foreground noise may very well be all the same for him. So if your communication is important, make sure you are getting through. And, despite what we are all told about a child with autism not being able to read facial expression, it was my experience with Pace that he certainly could!

Tip # 6: Know that he very much enjoys his classmates and they are capable of really liking him and can learn to deal with his most challenging behaviors.

Expect the other students to be kind, considerate and genuine friends with Pace. You won't be disappointed. Dr.Hiam Ginott, who wrote many books on how good relationships work, was right when he said the teacher sets the climate for each day in the classroom. Your attitude and reactions to any and all behaviors will be noted and adopted by the class. If the building happens to fall down around you, quietly begin to pick up bricks and stack them. The children will follow, and if you suggest that they classify them in a particular way, it will give them something to think about as you get things put back in place.

Just so with a child who is prone to meltdowns or disruptive behavior. Acknowledge it. Defuse it. Make it be something we live with and are getting very good at dealing with. Empower the children to know how to accept their classmate and help him be the best he can be. Let them experience the success and pride that comes with being a kind friend.

In closing, let me say that as Pace's classroom teacher, I have certainly gained new insight into how children learn. I have developed a great appreciation for and trust in the teachers with whom I have shared the experience. I have certainly been humbled. I have found peace with failed attempts, and I have found more rewards than I could have imagined. May you find as much fulfillment as I did as you continue this process that is, without a doubt, full of challenges but also full of good surprises and many wonders.

Wishing you every success,

Sherry Corden

P.S. Tip #7: Never allow the parents to schedule a meeting during prime academic time. This may be advantageous to them, but it is much to the detriment of every other child in the class who will not be receiving instruction from you while you are tied up in a meeting.

Parents' Perspective

How do we top such an incredible year? What can we do to keep the ball rolling? We met just about all of the goals we had set for Pace during the kindergarten year and saw some gains we never could have imagined. As it turned out, we needn't have worried. True to form, the Rocky Hill staff and experts had a game plan in mind.

They chose and assigned Pace to the first grade teacher who seemed the best match for him — one who had extensive experience with including special-needs children in her classroom and knew a good deal about autism. (Of course, as luck would have it, she left right before the school year started for a better job, but her replacement turned out to have many strengths, too.) The important thing is to try to place your child with someone who has the right chemistry and credentials to understand and be able to build on the progress of the previous year.

Our team created a six-week extended school year course to train Pace for the physical, academic, and social demands of first grade. We identified some key skills we wanted him to learn over the summer and developed a combined private therapy and home program to master those skills. The school team designed a special desk for Pace with a screen on three sides to cut down on distractions, a slanted surface for ease of writing, and pockets on either side which would hold folders labeled for work "to do," and work "completed."

We continued to chip away at self-care skills. We faded prompts and required more and more independence. We insisted on longer utterances and meaningful answers to questions. We gave him his own date book so that he could keep up with his own daily schedule (he wasn't yet writing, but he certainly could read entries we'd put in the date book for him). And finally, his Rocky Hill team of experts hand-picked a small group of close friends and other children with special needs from his kindergarten class to be placed in the next class with him so that he (and they) would have the comfort of familiar faces and a built-in support group. The good will that these children had shown Pace all through kindergarten and the subsequent friendships that had evolved were perhaps our strongest secret weapons for surviving the year ahead.

Having fun on field trips is a great way to cultivate friendships.

The peers have their say

Q: What advice would you give someone who might be in Pace's class next year?

Treat him like everybody else.

Wade M.

Be nice and play with him.

Peyton B.

Hang around him — take his hand.

Macy M.

It's a really hard responsibility to help him but you can do it. He's a really good kid — you just need to get to know him.

Jack R.

Spend some time with him and be nice.

Sam C.

Don't really push him because he doesn't mean to hit you and he's different from all of us and I think you should like that.

Morgan T.

If you want him to be friends, just be the friend you want *him* to be.

Manny R.

Q: If you could have one wish for Pace, what would it be?

I wish he would be in my class.

Parker M.

I wish he could run faster.

Ray B.

I wish he could talk and play with us and be rich and have friends.

Morgan T.

Rich means he has everything in his house.

Megan H.

I just want him to be happy.

Morgan T.

I wish he could talk.

Peyton B.

Flowers

I wish he could talk so he wouldn't be so frustrated and punch people and kick people anymore.

Sam C.

I wish the disease or whatever it is was gone. BOOM! And he could play with us, talk with us, and it would be easier to communicate.

Jack R.

School professionals and staff offer advice

Q: What advice would you give to those who will have Pace in school next year?

Never back him in a corner.

Guidance Counselor

Have high expectations. Set goals. Just because he has a disability doesn't mean that he can't successfully reach them!

Teachers' Assistant

Don't give up trying different strategies. What works for one child may not work for another and vice versa. Keep trying to find a motivator and understand the individual.

Occupational Therapist

Always look beyond the first impression. Jot down that first impression and keep a monthly two-sentence-length commentary so you can go back and review. Rely on more than your memory. There will be peaks and valleys, but concentrate on the peak times.

School Psychologist

Be patient. There is no limit to the gains that can be made if there is collaboration.

Principal

I would tell someone in a similar situation to have multiple people observe the student. It took a team effort to make Pace successful. Different observations and points of view helped shed light into his world.

CDC Case Manager

Make sure you communicate with all of the professionals working with the child on a consistent basis. Know what his day consists of. You must know how he is reacting to different situations all throughout the day. Know how the other professionals are communicating and what communication they are receiving from this child. Provide structure and communication aids for the child. It is critical! If something doesn't work, don't stay with it forever. Move on until you find something that does.

Speech Therapist

This job requires a lot of patience, understanding, and energy.

Teachers' Assistant

Be patient, be responsive, be flexible.

Librarian

Have high expectations. Don't tolerate aggressive behavior. Use rewards and consequences. Be patient, determined, and consistent.

Special Education Case Manager

Make it your personal goal to look past the behaviors — the apparent lack of interest in social interaction and any other superficial characteristics you may initially deem negative — and find out who the child inside really is and what you can do to make his life better!

Speech Therapist

Be willing to open up your mind and heart to the things that they (Pace and individuals with autism or developmental delays of any kind) can teach you, because not only will you learn a lot about them, but more often than not, they will teach you something about yourself — but only if you're willing.

School Nurse

Just follow Pace's lead and those of the other students to try to determine how best to explain something to him. Do not pity. Do not lower your standards. Rather, modify how you approach a concept or lesson.

Music Teacher

I would suggest teaching with the use of centers for Pace. Other children are great helpers and buddies for Pace to stay focused. I feel that it helps him to learn many tasks in a short period of time, along with auditory listening and visual cues.

Physical Education Instructor

Inclusion works well for Pace. However, when he becomes aggressive or disruptive to the regular program, he must be removed until behaviors are acceptable. He has come so far. We are seeing tremendous flexibility, more true communication — verbally and socially — more tolerance for non-preferred activities. Other kids in the school know, accept, and like him — tolerate his episodes.

Special Education Case Manager

Q: Did you learn anything new from being around Pace?

Absolutely! Each time a child "flowers" when there were some doubts about the possibility of improvement, it is always a new experience, because each child is so unique.

School Psychologist

He just reinforced the things that I already knew: that individuals are unique unto themselves, though they may have the same or similar diagnoses, exposures, problems, etc.

School Nurse

I learned to keep an open mind. And behavior *is* communication.

Speech Therapist

Never assume that a child does not understand. He may or may not, but talk to the child, not about him.

Occupational Therapist

He was exceptionally intelligent and able to understand (receive communication), to a much greater degree than I had expected or experienced with such children previously.

Principal

I learned that autistic children have different ways of reacting to situations. My husband and I are godparents of a four-year-old autistic girl who will be ours if anything happens to her parents. I need to know as much as possible for better understanding of autism so that I can be there for Elizabeth.

Librarian

Cherish each day in this world. Do whatever it takes to make another's life just a little bit more special, along with patience and understanding.

Physical Education Instructor

I know every child is different, but Pace allowed me to see within every child there are similarities to other children.

CDC Case Manager

I feel that in order for inclusion to work you need teachers and staff who are willing to work together. I believe that if the special-needs child becomes disruptive they should be removed until able to return to class just as you would do with any child. Inclusion also builds a compassionate, caring, and loving child. It helps all children to see that no matter what the limitations are, there are many things a special child can do and that they are just like any other child in many ways.

Teachers' Assistant

What the other parents thought

Pace was a wonderful reminder to me of the gift that every human being is on this earth. While each of us has our different glitches and imperfections, God has given us other lovable qualities. Pace has so many lovable qualities.

BR

Pace was such a smart and gifted child who had so much to share with and teach his classmates, who all accepted him for his unique little self!

DM

I think we all learned from Pace. I hope my son learned that there are many different kinds of people in the world — all special and created by God! I learned that Pace may communicate differently than some of the other children, yet he was far beyond his peers in reading, for instance.

SM

I will never forget one time when my daughter and I were in the car and she started telling me that Pace could read. This was amazing to her because she couldn't read yet at all, and in fact, was struggling very hard with it at the time. I was astonished, because I knew Pace still wasn't talking very much, and it was incredible to me that a child who had such a severe disability could be so far ahead of his peers in another area. I remember we were stopped at a red light when I heard my daughter say in a small voice from the back seat of the car "Momma, I wish God had made me like Pace."

I had to turn around in my seat and look at her. "Why, baby?" I asked. "Because then it wouldn't be so hard for me to read," she answered.

It was in that moment that I realized my daughter could not see Pace's disability at all, only his strength. And she was envious.

DM

Children with special needs can feel a part of and succeed in a regular classroom if they have the right teachers and atmosphere.

CG

I learned that just because a child has a learning impairment it does not mean that he or she is incapable of participating with the other students. I would say be open-minded about everyone and everything. And be kind. I always try to put myself on the opposite side and it helps me to understand a little more.

PR

I would encourage parents not to prejudge the situation. I would tell them what a positive experience we had with Pace.

SM

I was pretty familiar with autistic children. My sister-in-law teaches them in Georgia. What I learned was how sensitive my child is toward someone with special needs. The fear is with the parents, not the kids. I believe as long as special needs children do not keep my child from learning, it is a valuable experience to be with them. My oldest daughter learned a lot about caring at Rocky Hill through being friends with a child with Down Syndrome. She continued this friendship during middle school and now as a senior in high school. Life includes all types of people and how we can appreciate their attributes. God bless Pace.

HM

In our family we try to teach our children not to discriminate against anyone because of who they are or what they can or cannot do. I guess they are listening!

JH

Be so very thankful if you have a special-needs child in your class. But I also must point out that I think the integration works because of the one-on-one relationship of the "Mrs. Hodges" of the world. I cannot imagine what the classroom would have experienced last year had there not been Mrs. Corden, Mrs. Sanders, and Mrs. Hodge! I would also encourage a parent to teach their children what an opportunity it is to learn to be friends and classmates and buddies with a special-needs child. The opportunities for learning life-lessons are endless.

BR

If inclusion is an option, fight for it. The inclusion of a nonverbal child is a great experience for not only the child but for his or her classmates as well. However, I would also state that a teacher such as Mrs. Hodge is imperative for the success of this or a similar situation.

MB

Placing your child in a class with special-needs children is good for both students. They learn far more than the basic curriculum would ever teach. The more diversity of people your child is exposed to, the more he will be equipped to handle situations he faces in life with people.

LC

As much as Pace has learned from the children in Sherry's class, they also learned a lot from him. Thank you for giving our children the pleasure of knowing Pace and the opportunity for our kids to see up close that we are truly all the same.

DM

My advice to other parents would be to treat everyone the way you want your own children to be treated — especially if they were in the same situation as Pace.

JH

I would tell other parents to inform their child about the child with special needs (of any type) ahead of time, to encourage them to always treat the child kindly and not to be scared.

DM

We are all mothers who love their children, want the best for them, and want them to succeed. If there is anything I or my child can do to help a family, we want to do it.

MT

Another thing that I am reminded of and amazed about each year as my children have special-needs children in their classes is the energy that the parents of the special-needs children have. I often went home after the end of a class party or field trip knowing that my son could safely entertain himself for a while as I unwound, and I wondered "When does Mary get to unwind?" I feel concern for Mary and moms like her. When do they have "down time?" When do they have complete peace? Is there always tension and worrying? I just think about that a lot. I hope that God has extra special mercy for parents of special-needs kids. I find myself running into Mary or another mom like her and praying very quickly that something extra-wonderful happens during their day.

BR

Path

What can we do to insure success going forward?

We lived through this dreaded year, where everything seemed to hang in the balance. Now we prepare for the next challenge. As a team, we can face and master this challenge. Pace can master this challenge, I'm positive.

You know you're alive if you can learn. Even old dogs learn new tricks. Only dead dogs cannot.

Live to Learn, Learn to Live

Life is a series of challenges that lead us to learn. You can define life in these terms. You know you're alive if you can learn. Even old dogs learn new tricks. Only dead dogs cannot. Challenge, frustration, learning, and growth are ongoing processes that define life.

We prepare as best we can. As we proceed, we do so with an open mind and willingness, even eagerness, to be flexible.

Plug Into the Power of Planning

Just as we prepared for the last challenge, we prepare for the next. Careful planning is a part of this. We prepare as best we can. As we proceed, we do so with an open mind and willingness, even eagerness, to be flexible. The story we have presented shows that the preparation helped. Flexibility helped. Positive expectations helped even more. Pace succeeded in kindergarten because of planning, flexibility, and positive expectations.

What will make the next year go well? As you've come to know Sherry, you've seen that the teacher is key.

Choose an Appropriate Teacher

I often ask the current teacher to help pick the next teacher. The kindergarten teacher usually knows all the first-grade teachers well. She knows the qualities they each bring to the classroom. She knows the child and the type of teacher he or she needs.

Identify Key Characteristics

So, what are the characteristics that we should look for in a teacher for a child with autism? It helps if the classroom and the teacher are highly organized. Organized classrooms are predictable. Organized classrooms are quieter and less chaotic. These things are essential for a child who is trying to deal with the sensory jungle.

A calm, quiet, reassuring, firm approach also promotes the child's adaptation. Loud, angry, demanding voices do not. Look for a teacher who can maintain his or her sense of calmness. Consistency and firmness are predictable. Loud, emotional, and reactive responses are not.

It is important to have a teacher who appreciates and accepts individual differences. The teacher should *want* this child. The teacher should be expected to make this work.

The teacher must be willing to listen to others and must be willing to join the creative brainstorming process. A teacher who feels he or she is an expert will not be able to do this. The teacher who modestly asks for help makes a good team problem solver.

Look for Flexibility

Firmness does not mean inflexible. A skilled teacher will adapt his or her style to the needs of the child. A good teacher will experiment and will consistently and firmly implement the things that seem to work

Look for key skills that the child will need in the next classroom. Just as we did in preparing for kindergarten, look at key vocabulary and essential behaviors that will increase the likelihood of success.

The experimenting will be most productive if it is based in team problem solving. This means the teacher must be willing to listen to others and must be willing to join the creative brainstorming process. A teacher who feels he or she is an expert will not be able to do this. The teacher who modestly asks for help makes a good team problem solver. This type of teacher learns from other team members.

Some teachers feel they should already know what to do. They are resistant and defensive. We need openness and flexibility, not a strong ego. We need a teacher willing to learn. Hopefully, the receiving teacher will prepare over the summer. He or she will read about autism, and will attend workshops. The best first-grade teacher will be willing to learn from others, especially the kindergarten teacher and the parent.

Groom the Child for Success

Have the team identify the peers who are preferred by the child with autism. Find those who seek out the child with autism and have shown they like to interact with him or her. Look for relatively calm children who enjoy helping others.

Look carefully for these qualities in the receiving teacher, then look for key skills that the child will need in the next classroom. Just as we did in preparing for kindergarten, look at key vocabulary and essential behaviors that will increase the likelihood of success. Join the receiving teacher in an open discussion of her expectations. Boil these down to the smallest list possible. Set a plan to work toward these over the summer months, and then prepare the child for first grade using the techniques listed earlier for preparing the child for kindergarten.

Choose a Pod of Peers to Travel with the Child

Targeting key skills and selecting a teacher will help. So will selecting a peer group to stay with the child. Have the team identify the peers who are preferred by the child with autism. Find those who seek out the child with autism and have shown they like to interact with him or her. Look for relatively calm children who enjoy helping others. Look for children who might be willing to share the interests of the target child. Look for peers whose parents have shown an interest in this process. Plan to maintain this peer group for as long as possible, even into high school. Plan carefully and slowly; there is no need to rush now.

Practice Patience

Patience is repeatedly listed as a crucial characteristic of those involved in the process. Did you notice how often this was mentioned in the first part of this chapter and throughout this book? Change requires patience. Persistence requires patience. Learning requires patience. The child with autism requires patience. Optimism requires patience.

Visualize Progress

We must expect things to go well. This means there is no time or room for pity. Empathy helps; pity does not. Share the child's strengths and challenges, but do not feel sorry for him. Instead, work to support his strengths and address his challenges. But do not waste time on pity. Earlier you read the words of educators and parents telling us this. They told us to be open and accepting rather than dwelling on the unfairness of it all.

Pity assumes a sorrowful state. Pity prejudges and is pessimistic. What we need now is openness to growth and a belief in possibilities. We need a mobilization of resources to face the challenges of teaching. We need the willingness to teach and the willingness to learn how to do this best for this particular child. Teaching and learning are powerful and life giving and are based on assets. Pity is limiting and is focused on weaknesses and worst-case scenarios.

> **We must expect things to go well. This means there is no time or room for pity. Empathy helps; pity does not. Share the child's strengths and challenges, but do not feel sorry for him. Instead, work to support his strengths and address his challenges.**

Expect things to go wrong, and they will go wrong. Expect things to work, and they are more likely to work. Negative expectations limit growth. Positive expectations facilitate growth.

Let's gather strength from these miracles. This will let us tap into the power of optimism.

See the Strength in Weaknesses, the Commonality in Diversity

A child cannot have weaknesses without having strengths. He cannot have challenges without having opportunities. Can we find these strengths and opportunities? Let us persist until we do. Let us look for team players who naturally notice strengths and opportunities in the child, in the staff, in the school, and in the community. We must be positive about what we are doing.

Expect Improvement, Discover Greatness

Fill your mind with positive expectations. It's been proven again and again that if you expect things to go wrong, they will go wrong. But when you expect things to work, then they are more likely to work. Negative expectations limit growth. Positive expectations facilitate growth.

Expect challenges, certainly. Life requires it of us. But expect that we will overcome each challenge so that we can face the next challenges. Expect that challenges will lead to the miracles of learning and growth. It is a continual process that positive expectations facilitate.

Focus explicitly on positive expectations. We have come much further than Mary ever thought was possible. We will go much further next year, and further still the next year after that. Let's gather strength from these miracles. This will let us tap into the power of optimism. I am positive about this!

Inclusion is for everyone. It is for the child with autism, as well as the child with Attention Deficit Hyperactivity Disorder. It is for the language impaired and the learning disabled. It is for those who are gifted, those who are mentally challenged, and those who are both at the same time. It benefits all children. It benefits the "typically developing" child, who learns to accept diversity and who learns to value individual gifts and challenges. It is for the parent of these peers. From their children they learn not to fear differences or the unknown that comes with differences. Inclusion is for educators who find they change the world by valuing and teaching every child in it. Inclusion is for everyone. The question we have strived to answer is not about whether to include or who to include; it is about how to include all. Join us!

Epilogue

The night before kindergarten started I remember looking at Pace as he slept and thinking, "Wow, this is either going to be life-altering in a good way, and bring this kid out of his shell, or it is going to be a total bust and do us all in."

And then I began to think about how I would have to guess how every day in kindergarten was. He would never tell me, because he couldn't. He couldn't comment on a beautiful sunset, share a sudden thought, wonder about the mysteries of life, tell me his dreams, or let me know if he was nervous, scared, or even if his stomach hurt.

I longed for one spontaneous word. Call me from another room. Yell at your sister. Say, "God bless you!" when I sneeze. Say, "I love you," when I do something nice. He had never said he loved me. And I had spent so much time, energy, money, sweat, tears, and endless, endless worry on him. Thoughts of his welfare consumed me. My heart was always full of feeling for him. Aware of his courage. Aware of his vulnerability. Aware of his potential. My heart.

I leaned down and laid my ear on his chest. His heart spoke to me in strong, regular beats. I could hear that. I could believe each beat held love for me. I could take that as clear affirmation that as long as that heart was beating it was sending a message of love.

I love you, Mommy. I love you, Mommy.

I could hear that.

It was beyond words.

Appendix

Pace's introduction book format 142

Pace's introduction book reprint 146

20 questions for your prospective kindergarten teacher 152

Sherry's rules 154

Daily report form 155

Daily schedule 156

Reward board 158

Social story for field trip 159

Social story for desired behavior 160

A typical day in kindergarten and how to get through it 161

Introduce your child with a simple, homemade picture book

Almost every kindergarten class has a low bookshelf accessible to everyone in the room at all times, that usually has a collection of picture books and stories of interest or educational value to the students. A simple book can be made at home to introduce your special child to the community of people who will coexist with him in his new classroom. It is a great and subtle way to gently instruct his peers in the things that make him different, that set him off or turn him on, and also the things that make him just like everybody else in the room. The following outline can be used to create a book that is unique to your own child. We suggest that you prepare it before school starts, share it with the teacher, and ask her or him to read it to the class early on and then place it on the common bookshelf and let it stay there available to anyone who is curious (including visitors, parents of other children in the class, teaching assistants, and professional observers) for the rest of the year.

NOTE: You can use either photographs of your child and things from his life that illustrate each page or have a sibling or friend make drawings.

We have reproduced the book that our family created for Pace the year he entered kindergarten so that you can see just how simple it can actually be.

COVER
WITH TITLE THAT INCLUDES CHILD'S NAME

PAGE 1: Hi! My name is _____

PAGE 2: I live with my _____ and _____ and
_____ in a nice _____.

(Name everyone who lives with the child, including pets, and show a picture of the place in which you live.)

PAGE 3: I like my _____very much!

(Choose a pet or favorite family member.)

PAGE 4: I like to _____.

(Name a favorite activity.)

PAGE 5: I like to _____.

(Name another favorite activity.)

PAGE 6: I like the _____.

(Name a favorite place.)

PAGE 7: And I love _____!

(Name something the child really loves.)

PAGE 8: Right now I don't say many words.

(Find a photo that shows the child looking contemplative or vulnerable.)

PAGE 9: But I am saying more words every day.

(Show the child with an object he can name and put in a caption that is something like, "Say, _____!")

PAGE 10: Some words mean a lot.

(Put together a collage of picture symbols that have meaning for your child like, "Oreo," "pizza," "McDonalds," "park," "swing," "read," "computer," and so on.)

PAGE 11: When I really like something I will _____ or
_____.

(We put, "flap my hands," and "flick my lips," in the spaces.)

PAGE 12: When I get angry sometimes I don't have the words I need.

(We used the picture symbol for "mad," and drew jets of steam coming out the ears.)

PAGE 13: So I may ____ or _____ or _____. Please tell me to stop.

(Use the picture symbols for "hit," or "kick," or "butt my head," and then the symbol for "STOP!" at the end.)

PAGE 14: Hold my hands and say, "I don't like that!" in a serious voice. That should help.

(Use the picture symbol for "I don't like that.)

PAGE 15: I love to laugh, and I like people,

(Use the picture symbol for "funny," and find a photo of your child in a situation in which he or she is having a great time.)

PAGE 16: But, sometimes I need my space.

(The picture symbol for "I need a break," works well here.)

PAGE 17: Sometimes I am afraid to try new things. So I watch a long time, and then I try.

(Picture symbols for "I don't know," "scared," "quiet," and "I like that," at the end illustrate this just fine, or you might be fortunate enough to have a photo of your child attempting to approach something of which he or she is unsure.)

PAGE 18: Sometimes loud or screechy noises make me mad or sad.

(You can use picture symbols for "loud," or "noisy," or cut out illustrations from a magazine of noisy things.)

PAGE 19: Just give me a little time to get myself back on track. Say, "It's ok."

(Find a photo of your child in a serene moment.)

PAGE 20: I love to learn.

(Show a photo of your child in a learning situation — maybe at speech therapy or OT.)

PAGE 21: I am happy to be at _____ school.

(Take a photo of your school.)

PAGE 22: And look forward to sharing happy times with new friends!

(You can show your child's new teacher and teacher's aide — if he/she has one — and something wonderful from the classroom.)

Pace's kindergarten introduction book

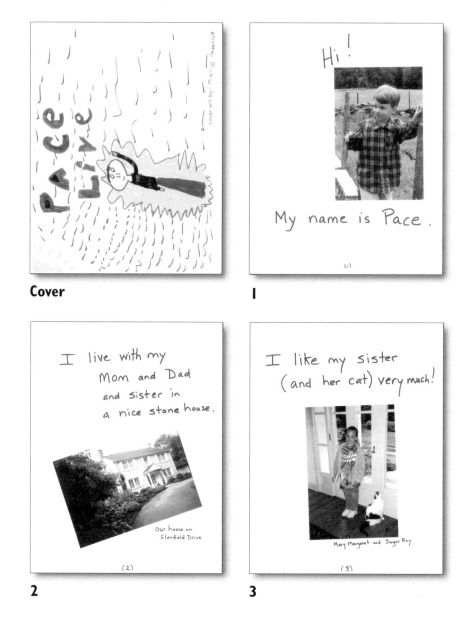

Cover

1

2

3

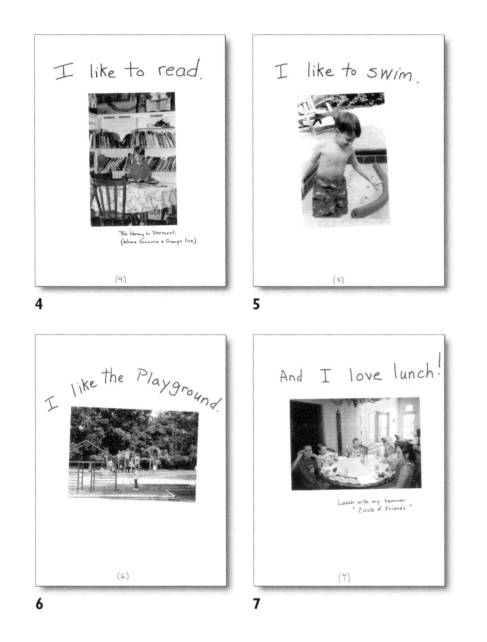

4

I like to read.

The library in Vermont.
(where Grammie + Grampa live)

(4)

5

I like to swim.

(5)

6

I like the Playground.

(6)

7

And I love lunch!

Lunch with my summer
" Circle of Friends "

(7)

Right now, I don't say many words.

(8)

8

But I am saying more words every day.

Say, "Dinosaur!"

(9)

9

Some words mean alot

OREO

train

park   lake

computer

swing   book   outside

slide

read   gym

bubbles

music

please   thank you

bathroom

(10)

10

When I really like something

I will flap my hands
or
"flick" my lips with
my fingers.   (11)

11

12 Or look at it out of the corner of my eye.

"Wow! Look at all those strawberries Grammie picked!"

(12)

13 when I get angry

Sometimes I don't have the words I need,

(13)

14 So, I may hit or kick or butt my head.

kick

mad

Please tell me to

stop

(14)

15 Hold my hands and say,

" I don't like that! "

i don't like that

in a serious voice. That should help.

(15)

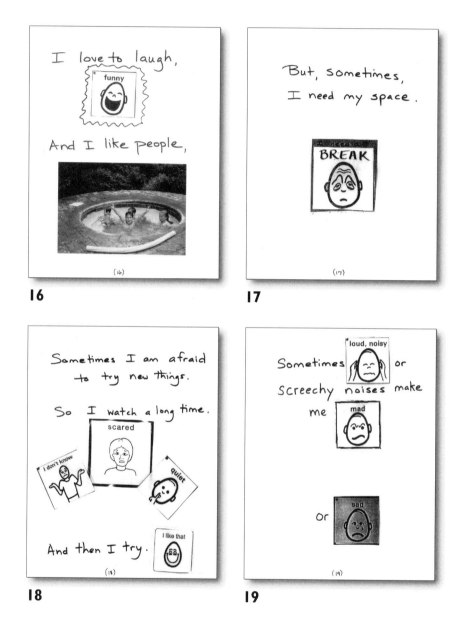

I love to laugh,

funny

And I like people,

(16)

16

But, sometimes,
I need my space.

BREAK

(17)

17

Sometimes I am afraid
to try new things.

So I watch a long time.

scared

I don't know

quiet

And then I try.

I like that

(18)

18

Sometimes loud, noisy or
Screechy noises make
me mad

or sad

(19)

19

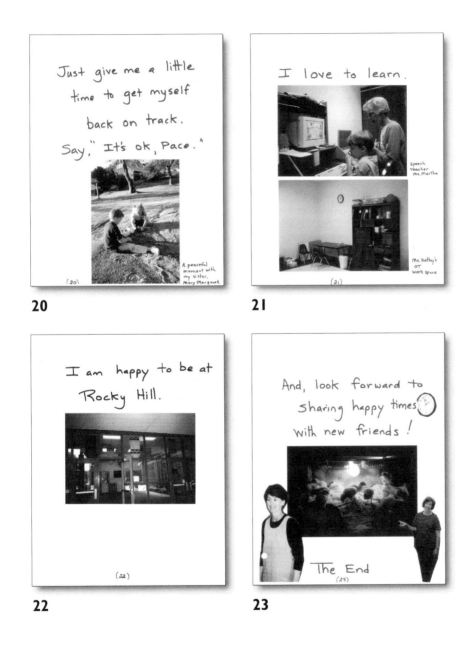

20

Just give me a little time to get myself back on track. Say," It's ok, Pace."

(20)

A peaceful moment with my sister, Mary Margaret

21

I love to learn.

Speech teacher Ms. Martha

Ms. Kathy's OT work space

(21)

22

I am happy to be at Rocky Hill.

(22)

23

And, look forward to sharing happy times with new friends!

The End

(23)

20 questions for your prospective kindergarten teacher

Please note: The following list of questions is provided for use as conversation starters by the parent-teacher team as they become acquainted. Some may already be answered without being asked. Some may come up spontaneously. Some will require explicit discussion.

Have you ever had a student with a communication disorder in your classroom?

How much do you feel you know about teaching such children?

Are you willing to attend workshops available through the school system to learn more about communication disorders? If all your costs were covered, would you attend workshops led by other organizations that specialize in this disorder?

Would you like suggestions on books that might be helpful to you in understanding this impairment? Would you be open to learning behavior management/teaching techniques from private professionals in this area?

Does anything about a child with a communication disorder worry you/scare you/turn you off? In what way?

Do you see the placement of a child with a communication disorder in your classroom as a hardship or an opportunity?

What adaptations (academic and social) would you be willing to make so that the child is included and can remain in the classroom as much as possible?

What do you foresee as trouble spots in the classroom, on the playground, at special events, on field trips, in the cafeteria?

Since children with communication disorders are sometimes virtually nonverbal and incapable of reporting, what can you do to keep parents informed of the child's life at school on a daily basis?

How will you present the child's differences to the other children in the class-room and what will you do if his/her behavior is frightening/disruptive/confusing?

What are your goals for children with communication disorders?

What are these children's limitations and what things do you assume they will never be able to do?

How would you assist the "special" teachers in having the most positive impact on this child (P.E., music, art, computer, library)?

How would you keep this child engaged and learning up to his/her potential, especially if he/she is passive/quiet/likes to keep to himself or herself?
How will you handle times of noncompliance?

What will you do if children in the classroom or others in the school tease/make fun of/shun this child?

Even though you don't really know this particular child yet, can you speculate on some of the positive influences he/she may have on your classroom?

How do you feel about having other children with special needs in your classroom along with a child or children with communication difficulties? How many could you accept and would it make a difference if their challenges were similar to or different that the ones presented by the child with communication impairment?

How would you like the classroom to be staffed? Should there be anyone dedicated solely to being the communication-impaired child's aide?

What would be the best way to schedule Occupational Therapy/Speech Therapy/Physical Therapy sessions that are required for the communication-impaired child?

Sherry's Rules

Always demonstrated with the physical cues indicated.

1. Follow the teacher's first request.
(Scooping motion of closed hand with index finger pointed upward.)

2. Keep your hands and feet to yourself.
(Hands and feet splayed out, then folded in.)

3. Ignore inappropriate behavior.
(Exaggerated motion of head turned to profile with eyes closed and nose in the air.)

4. Walk and talk quietly.
(Elaborate tip-toe.)

5. Raise your hand to speak.
(Left hand raised. Right index finger to lips.)

Daily report form

(This was usually filled out by the teacher's assistant.)

Date_____

I had a good / OK / not so good morning.
I had a good / OK / not so good afternoon.

I went to PE / Library / Music / Computer
I participated ___yes ___no

I had OT / Speech / PT today. We did _____

I had _____ for snack.
I ate all / some / no snack.

I chose _____ for lunch.
I ate all / some / no lunch.

I showed good / some / little effort this morning.
I showed good / some / little effort this afternoon.

My behavior was good / average / poor this morning.
Hitting / head butting / kicking / yelling / other_____

My behavior was good / average / poor this afternoon.
Hitting / head butting / kicking / yelling / other_____

I used the bathroom ___yes ___no
Please list times and results _____

At recess, I _____

Comments _____
_____
_____
_____
_____

Daily schedule board

Detailed schedule

As activities are completed picture symbols can be taken off and stored in an envelope or plastic baggie affixed to the back of the schedule board. "Reward" cards for work done may be placed in the three empty places shown and used as work is completed during the day.

Simplified schedule

The daily schedule can be streamlined for children who don't need or can't handle as much detail as shown on the previous page. In this case, as activities are done, the picture is moved to the second ("done") line of velcro. When work is complete, the child may choose from the rewards on the bottom line.

Task/Reward board

Pace's Work Contract

3 stars = Free Choice Box
5 stars = Computer or Playtime
8 stars = Video and Popcorn

	Good Behavior	Work by myself or with little help	Work done before timer goes off
Red Folder	⭐	⭐	⭐
Blue Folder	⭐	⭐	⭐
Green Folder	⭐	⭐	⭐
Yellow Folder	⭐	⭐	⭐
Orange Folder	⭐	⭐	⭐

Social story for field trip

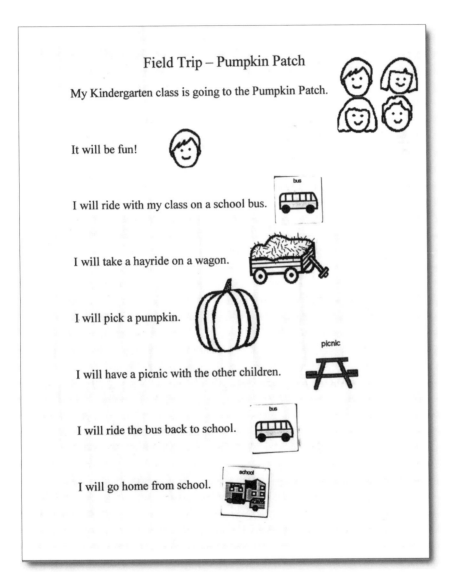

Field Trip – Pumpkin Patch

My Kindergarten class is going to the Pumpkin Patch.

It will be fun!

I will ride with my class on a school bus.

I will take a hayride on a wagon.

I will pick a pumpkin.

I will have a picnic with the other children.

I will ride the bus back to school.

I will go home from school.

Social story for desired behavior

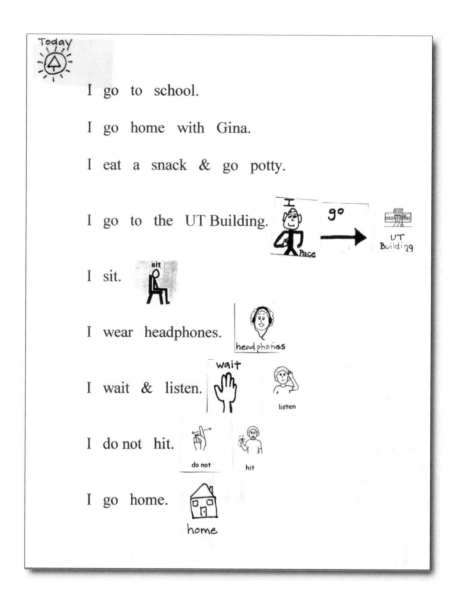

A typical day in kindergarten and how to get through it.

By Sherry Henshaw Corden

Arrival:

At Rocky Hill, children arriving in cars go to the car lobby, are organized into class groups, and wait until the bell rings and it is time to proceed to their class-rooms. Those arriving by bus go to the bus room and follow the same proce-dure. Both areas are crowded and loud. Many directives are given to the groups. Some are visual. Most are verbal. It was decided that Pace would do better if he bypassed the car lobby and went directly to the resource room until time for school to begin. Since he was a boy who clearly craved order, peace and quiet, it seemed foolish to start his day in a chaotic environment. His aide, Mrs. Hodge, watched for the class to walk by the resource room and then would assist him in joining the group. Later, that early morning time slot was used by the OT to allow Pace to swing in her room.

Entry:

The classroom is clearly marked with a distinctive mailbox outside the door. Initially a picture schedule was placed beside the mailbox to remind Pace of the morning routine which outlined these steps:

- ☞ Put notes from home in the mailbox
- ☞ Put lunch money in the lunch money drawer
- ☞ Put coats and backpacks in the cubby
- ☞ Stop and answer a question on a graph using a Unifix cube
- ☞ Sign in by tracing your name on a paper we supply each day
- ☞ Vote for the book of your choice for the after-lunch story
- ☞ Choose a book to read from the bookcase and find your assigned seat on the carpet.

What a list of things to do! It was found that he didn't need a schedule. All sta-tions followed a logical path that never changed. Mrs. Hodge prompted him through the routine at first but it soon became a natural part of him, as it does with all the children.

Group Time:

Morning group time begins with a joyful song that includes movement. With Mrs. Hodge prompting, Pace participated from the beginning. It was obvious that it felt good to him to be a part of that, and that made it clear that music would be a way to bring him to the carpet and transition him from place to place and activity to activity in general. The special education aide has a key role in all adaptations that are made for children with special needs. He or she is closest to the child and can watch for areas of challenge and opportunity, then offer assistance where it is needed and take advantage of motivators for desirable behavior as they are revealed

Communication During Morning Ritual:

When addressing children, especially children with communication disorders, use everything you have! There is the verbal message, of course, but the tone should clearly tell if it is an order or a choice or if pleasure or displeasure is being expressed. And then the body language — which can really work — the body language can often express the thought without any words at all. One's eyes in particular, one's mouth, the position of one's shoulders and head, the way one sits in the chair; all of these speak volumes. And even though it had been reported that Pace would not register these things, it was found that he did and that they were as effective in controlling his behavior as they were with the other children.

Acceptable Behavior and Positioning During Morning Ritual:

While it is expected that all students face the teacher during group time, Pace would often turn his back. It was soon realized that that was okay and that he was definitely still attending and might even have been able to attend better without the added visual stimulation. Rather than get him to comply with a lot of demands right at the start, one objective was chosen — getting him to stay on his carpet square during group time — and the aim was to fulfill that one objective only. He was bored with most of the conversation during this time and wanted a book to look at, but that escape wasn't allowed. There was a container of Thera-Putty on the shelf behind him and he was given permission to manipulate that, which did help him to stay put and sit quietly. Compromise!

Participation in Morning Ritual:

Pace was always offered his turn during calendar time. In the beginning he sometimes would not participate, and often Mrs. Hodge would assist him. The other children would verbally encourage him and applaud when he did fulfill a task. In time, he grew to love taking his turn. Even though his back was usually turned, it was clear he was listening. It was apparent that he probably could read his name on the helper's chart, and anticipate when his turn was coming because one time when his job was accidentally skipped over he became extremely upset and would not calm down until he was allowed to perform his task.

Facilitating Transitions:

Sturdy colored tape and footprints placed on permanent lines on the floor help with lining up, putting away lunch money, getting a drink at the water fountain, and waiting in the lunch line. Each activity has a corresponding color that can be easily adapted to a picture communication card. The red line is for lining up. Footprints are at the head of each line and the leader stands on these with all the rest of the children falling in behind. A green line shows the way to the water fountain and a blue line indicates the path to putting away lunch money. In the cafeteria there are two sets of footprints, because there is a double line.

Everyone uses these tape lines. They keep children from spilling out into the hall when the class is preparing to travel to another destination, they clearly show where each child should be, and because of them, there is far less scuffling. Incidentally, there is a space between the footprints and the beginning of the tape line which helps to develop a sense of personal space.

Setting Boundaries:

Large red circles mean stop, just like a traffic light. Red circles are placed on every single thing that should not be touched. They have even been placed under tables for the benefit of one child we had one year who liked to hide under the tables instead of doing his work. This is a clear visual cue and also eliminates having to put away or hide cumbersome objects the children are not equipped to use just yet. Smaller circles of other various colors are used to label games, toys, and Work Jobs so they can be easily put away in their proper places on the shelves that are also marked with corresponding circles.

Small Group Instruction:

This was the most difficult time for Pace. Paper and pencil work was definitely a non-preferred activity for him so another way had to be found to teach the skill. One alternative was to use a Work Job. These are highly manipulative activities that are organized in individual tubs and stored on shelves around the room. Generally, kindergarteners use Work Jobs for independent drill and practice. Each child will take a tub to a private spot on the floor and complete it. The child then raises his or her hand for an adult to check the work and register a score and a comment in the child's work record book.

Since he was more attracted to manipulatives than the pencil and paper work, a Work Job was pulled for Pace that addressed the skill being taught and he was allowed to practice the skill that way. In the beginning he needed a secluded area in which to perform these tasks, but as time went on he was able to transition to a more central place on the floor, and then finally, to the table with the other children.

Another typical variation to adapt work for Pace was the way Pictionary was approached. Each child has a Pictionary notebook in which he or she draws each week. For instance, over the course of a week a child will draw several pictures of words beginning with a "b" for the "Bb" page. Since Pace was not drawing yet he was allowed to select "b" pictures from a set of precut pictures that featured "b" words as well as pictures of things that began with one or two other sounds. This would at least give him practice in sounding out the letter, identifying words that did or did not begin with the letter, and gluing pictures onto his pages.

Finishing Work:

Having more than one activity to complete was a challenge and one of the best solutions for getting Pace to work evolved from this situation. The enormous Picture Exchange Communication System (PECS) book with which he had begun the year was just too cumbersome and inefficient for spontaneous, every-day use. So, a simple clip board was devised that was light, easy, and flexible, and allowed a clear visual to be set up for expectations of Pace and the rewards he might earn for desirable behavior. It had a "To Do" line and a "Finished" line, and a "Reward" line at the bottom. All these lines were Velcro. A set of cards was placed on the "To Do" line which showed the work he needed to finish and as each job was completed he moved the card down to the "Finished" line. When all the cards were moved he was then allowed to choose a card from the reward line and immediately go enjoy that activity. These would be short, simple rewards like "Swing," "Jump," "Book," or "Treat Box." An activity which required more time, like the computer, would be saved for a free-time period or the end of the day.

Lunch:

The children are asked to get their lunches out of their cubbies if they bring lunch, and retrieve their lunch money if they buy lunch. Then they gather on the group time rug and remain silent while they are shown one child's name at a time from a stack. As each child reads his or her name he or she silently lines up on the colored line at the door. Pace's ability for visual recognition and memory allowed him to be one of the first to read not only his name, but everyone else's name as well. This was a wonderful moment for him and the other children when they were able to appreciate a strength he had.

There was not much need to adapt the usual lunchtime routine for Pace. Even though the cafeteria is noisy and full of sensory input, lunchtime is also highly ritualized and therefore probably one of the more comforting parts of the day for Pace.

Second Group Time:

Often "Daily News" is shared at this time. Initially, since Pace was virtually non-verbal, his mother provided news to be shared about Pace and this was verbalized and written for him on the black board. Eventually, he could read what had been written to some degree, and even write some words by tracing over a simple sentence written with a "water pen." By the way, a water pen is really just a stamp moistener. It works like a charm. Evaporation is magic for kindergarteners, and once the water has evaporated there is no visible sign that the child required any assistance.

Play Time:

The playground was a wonderful place for the children to model physical activities, interact socially with Pace, and learn some new ways to have fun from him. It was amazing how persistent the children were in trying to get Pace to play with them and how very aware they were of his safety and whereabouts. Pace was never allowed to wander off. Someone always had his hand, usually one on each side, and if he did not line up with the group when it was time to go, someone would always retrieve him without even being asked. He took all this in stride and seemed to enjoy the closeness of friends outside. Although he was not particularly athletic or daring, he did like to experience certain sensations. A lot was learned about Pace's ability to maintain balance in precarious positions and several of us nearly had heart attacks in the beginning of the year as we watched him anxiously from below — ready to catch him if necessary — as he teetered at the edge of a high platform that housed the "fireman's pole." But he never fell, and this encounter with possible danger must have lost its luster because he eventually stopped doing it.

Free Choice:

Left to his own devices, Pace was almost always drawn to solitary activities like reading a book or playing on the computer. It would have been preferable for Pace to use this time to interact with the other children but he was reluctant to do so and almost never initiated even parallel play with anyone else. So a way was found to put him into more social situations by letting him "choose" a friend to accompany him to the resource room where he could play a supervised board game or engage in some kind of play activity that would encourage communication and sharing. Now, Pace was not going to spontaneously "choose" anyone. A way was needed to stimulate this action and give him ownership of the outcome, so a system was devised where cards were presented to him with the names of about three of his classmates and he was asked to pick one. He liked doing this and his decisions were always deliberate and meaningful. It became a status position to be chosen, just like the cookie jar that only occasionally comes down from the top shelf. The selectiveness, infrequency and anticipation of being chosen made this a much sought after honor. This has always been Dana Kenny's (the Special Education Case Manager) way of facilitating interaction among children of differing learning styles and is certainly one reason why the special education program at Rocky Hill is so successful, so inclusive, so accepted by parents and typically developing children.

Special Areas:

With activities like gym, music, guidance, or library, Pace usually went along with the class and participated up to his comfort level. He was always accompanied by an aide and occasionally had to be pulled out from the class if his behavior became too disruptive. These were the least structured and most unpredictable times for the children and the special area teachers had varying degrees of success with and confidence in their ability to deal with Pace's communication challenges. It was found that a visual support like a schedule board with pictures that outlined the expectations involved was very helpful. This also applied to assemblies, field trips, vision/hearing tests, and other out-of-the-ordinary activities as well. Social Stories work wonders as "stage setters." They are invaluable.

Snack:

In hot weather popsicles and juice were often given to the children outside, and Pace enjoyed those. If the snack was served inside and was not to his liking, often he would sit at the table with the other children and not partake of the treat being offered. That was really alright, and wasn't a concern. Almost every year there are one or two children who choose not to snack. The most difficult part was explaining to all the parents who supplied the treats that it wasn't that Pace didn't like the things they offered, it was probably just that he was on sensory overload and didn't feel like adding to it by eating. Most of them didn't take it personally. The best part was that it was very important to all parents that Pace be included and his food preferences, if he had them, not be overlooked.

Preparation for Departure:

All the children were instructed to clean up from having their snack, get their backpacks out of the cubbies, and sit quietly on the group rug while their names were called for pick up by their parents. The students in Pace's class had the luxury of being at the end of the building and could leave directly from the classroom, out a side door, down some steps and out to the car line where they would be assisted into their parents' cars by a teacher. Pace's mom always parked out front and came to the room to pick up Pace, because that kept him from waiting too long with a wiggling group of restless children at the end of a full day. We always managed a friendly greeting, but avoided any lengthy exchange about the day, because a daily report was sent home in Pace's backpack every day, which usually provided plenty of details.

One of the most effective programs that Rocky Hill recently integrated into our kindergarten curriculum is the SMART program, which stands for Stimulating Maturity through Accelerated Reading Readiness Training. I did not go into detail about this portion of our day because each school will have its own way of using the program and what we did may not be pertinent to another school's situation at all. So suffice it to say, that this is an excellent enrichment that worked very well for us and we urge you to use the contact information below and explore how it might work for you.

Developed by the Minnesota Learning Resource Center, the SMART program is a powerful method of producing higher levels of pre-academic readiness and early academic achievement by enhancing many typical school activities with brain stimulation components to boost performance. Training for SMART is offered during a three-to-five day workshop/seminar to school teams consisting of administrators, kindergarten and/or first-grade teachers, special-needs teachers and staff, and physical education teachers. The program consists of three sets of activities located in three areas: desk activities, floor activities, and playground or gym activities. The curriculum relates to the academic areas of language development, second language exposure, pre-reading, early reading and reading, pre-math, early arithmetic and arithmetic, pre-writing and writing, physiologic readiness, coordination and attention. SMART has been used in alternate-day, half-day, and all-day kindergarten settings, first and second grades, and after-school and summer remedial/compensatory boost-up programs. It is a fantastic program and has great benefits for all children, no matter what their learning style may be!

Contact: Minnesota Learning Resource Center at ACTG@mail.actg.org
Or write: A Chance to Grow, Inc., New Visions School, 1800 Second Street N.E., Minneapolis, Minnesota, 55418, and ask for information on the SMART program.

Resources

Ayers, A.J. (1979). *Sensory Integration and the Child.* Los Angeles: Western Psychological Services.

Ginott, Haim G. (1993). *Teacher and Child.* New York: 1st Collier Books.

Hay, Louise L. (audio programs – various dates). *Life! Reflections on Your Journey, Morning and Evening Meditations, Overcoming Fears, The Power is Within You, What I Believe.* Carlsbad, CA: Hay House Inc.

Hay, Louise L. (1984). *You Can Heal Your Life.* (Includes CD) Carlsbad, CA: Hay House Inc.

Hay, Louise L. (2004). *I Can Do It.* (Includes CD) Carlsbad, CA: Hay House, Inc.

Kranowitz, C. S. (1998). *The Out-of-Sync Child: Recognizing and Coping with Sensory Integration Dysfunction.* New York: Skylight Press.

Lee, Cyndi (2004). *Meditations for Balance and Joy.* New York: OM Yoga Center (www.omyoga.com or www.therelaxationcompany.com).

Moor, J. (2002). *Playing, Laughing and Learning with Children on the Autism Spectrum: A Practical Resource of Play Ideas for Parents and Carers.* London: Jessica Kingsley Publishers.

National Research Council (2001). *Educating Children with Autism.* Committee on Educational Interventions for Children with Autism. Catherine Lord and James P. McGee, eds. Division of Behavioral and Social Sciences and Education. Washington, DC: National Academy Press.

Sonders, S. A. (2002). *Giggle Time – Establishing the Social Connection: A Program to Develop the Communication Skills of Children with Autism.* London: Jessica Kingsley Publishers.

Utley, C. A. & Mortweet, S. L. (1997). Peer-mediated instruction and interventions. *Focus on Exceptional Children.* 29 (5), pp 1-23.

William Allen, Ph.D., is a developmental psychologist licensed in Tennessee. He has over 20 years experience in working with children with autism, their parents, and their teachers. Dr. Allen is a strong believer in the developmental potential of children, and in the power of optimism and positive expectations. He travels around the country conducting training in autism, child development and integrated health care. Dr. Allen lives in rural East Tennessee with his wife and three children. Away from work he relaxes by hiking in the Great Smoky Mountains National Park, and by learning to play the harp guitar.

Sherry Henshaw Corden (above right) has been teaching kindergarten at Rocky Hill Elementary School in Knoxville, Tennessee, for two decades. She is a product of the Knoxville/Knox County Public School system and holds a Bachelor of Science Degree in Elementary Education from the University of Tennessee. A strong advocate for inclusion and champion of all children, Ms. Corden typically welcomes around five students with significant physical or learning challenges into her classroom every year. Aside from her work at school she also enjoys the company of friends, the closeness of family, and the delight of being a grandmother.

Mary Donnet Johnson (above center) grew up in Vermont, earned a B.A. at Sarah Lawrence College, and spent ten years in New York City as a professional actress. She then emigrated to the South and applied her talents to a second career as a writer, director, and producer of broadcast commercials and other corporate communication materials. Now married with two young children, Mary has settled in East Tennessee where she spends most of her time guiding and supporting the academic and leisure-time activities of her children while pursuing a third (and very rewarding) career as a writer and publisher of helpful books on autism and related special needs.

Pace Johnson is a rising third-grader with autism and has been fully included in regular public school classrooms since kindergarten. He most recently portrayed Thomas Edison in the second grade wax museum, gave an oral report on contrasting habitats to his entire class, and personally sent Valentines to nearly 30 friends, teachers, and classmates last spring. Pace loves animals, books, and the computer, and looks forward to the adventures, challenges, and triumphs awaiting him in the years ahead.